The Catholic Answer

BOOK
of
MARY

VERY REVEREND
PETER M.J. STRAVINSKAS,
PH.D., S.T.D.

OUR SUNDAY VISITOR PUBLISHING DIVISION
OUR SUNDAY VISITOR, INC.
HUNTINGTON, INDIANA 46750

Table of Contents

Part 2: Doctrine

Part 3: Apologetics

Part 4: Marian Prayer and Devotion

Contributors

THE VERY REV. PETER M. J. STRAVINSKAS, PH.D., S.T.D., is the editor of *The Catholic Answer* and the founding superior of the Diocesan Oratory of St. Philip Neri in the Diocese of Scranton, Pennsylvania.

MR. DAVE ARMSTRONG is a convert from Evangelicalism. He writes from Detroit, Michigan.

THE REV. RICHARD BRADFORD is a convert from Anglicanism and the chaplain of the Congregation of St. Athanasius in Boston, a community of the Anglican Use in the Catholic Church.

THE REV. PETER JOHN CAMERON, O.P., is professor of homiletics at St. Joseph Seminary in Yonkers, New York, and editor-in-chief of *Magnificat*. He is the author of *To Praise, To Bless, To Preach,* published by Our Sunday Visitor, Inc.

THE REV. ROMANUS CESSARIO, O.P., is a professor of systematic theology at St. John's Seminary in Boston, Massachusetts.

MR. STEVEN COLLISON works as a computer programmer. He writes from Old Saybrook, Connecticut.

MR. JEFFERY DENNIS studied at Olivet Nazarene College, Indiana University, and the University of Notre Dame. A freelance writer and adjunct professor of English, he writes extensively on biblical and theological subjects.

THE REV. CHARLES DICKSON is a Lutheran pastor, college chemistry professor, and author of *A Protestant Pastor Looks at Mary*, published by Our Sunday Visitor , Inc.

THE REV. GILES DIMOCK, O.P., with a doctorate in sacred theology from the Pontifical University of St. Thomas Aquinas in Rome, currently serves on the Pontifical Faculty of the Immaculate Conception in Washington, D.C.

SISTER MADELEINE GRACE, C.V.I., holds a doctorate in historical theology and teaches at the University of St. Thomas and Our Lady of the Lake Weekend College in Houston, Texas.

THE REV. NICHOLAS GREGORIS is a member of the Diocesan Oratory of St. Philip Neri in Mount Pocono, Pennsylvania. He has earned degrees from Seton Hall University, the Pontifical Gregorian University, and the Pontifical Faculty Marianum in Rome.

DR. KEVIN ORLIN JOHNSON is the author of *Rosary: Mysteries, Meditations and the Telling of the Beads,* published by Pangaeus Press.

THE REV. DR. DONALD LACY is a minister of the United Methodist Church and a frequent contributor to efforts for the advancement of ecumenical dialogue and Christian unity.

THE REV. PAUL D. LEE is director of ecumenical and interreligious affairs for the Archdiocese of Washington.

THE REV. TERRIL D. LITTRELL is a Methodist minister and pastor of the Bluff City United Methodist Church, Bluff City, Tennessee.

DR. LEON MCKENZIE is the author of *Pagan Resurrection Myths and the Resurrection of Jesus*, published by Bookwrights Press.

THE REV. JAY SCOTT NEWMAN is a convert to Catholicism and a priest of the Diocese of Charleston, holding a licentiate in canon law from the Pontifical Gregorian University in Rome.

MISS MARGARET O'CONNELL, who writes and works in her native New York City, is a senior research editor and a member of the Catholic Press Association.

MRS. CATHERINE M. ODELL is the author of *Faustina* and *Those Who Saw Her*, both published by Our Sunday Visitor, Inc.

BROTHER ANTHONY M. OPISSO, a convert from Judaism, has been a hermit since 1964, living under obedience to the abbot of Our Lady of Calvary Abbey near Rogersville, New Brunswick, Canada.

THE REV. JACOB RESTRICK, O.P., a convert from Anglicanism, is a member of the St. Joseph Province of the Dominican Order, with a licentiate in sacred theology from the Pontifical Faculty of the Immaculate Conception in Washington, D.C.

THE REV. BONAVENTURE STEFUN, O.F.M CONV., has served as an editor for various publications of his religious community and as a hospital chaplain for the past several years.

MR. ROBERT SUNGENIS, a former Evangelical minister, is the author of several apologetical works, including *Not by Faith Alone: A Biblical Study of the Catholic Doctrine of Justification* by Queenship Publishing.

SISTER MARIANNE LORRAINE TROUVÉ, F.S.P., has served in Boston, New York, Miami, New Orleans, and Toronto, where she has carried out the evangelization efforts of the Daughters of St. Paul.

THE REV. WILLIAM WEARY is a priest of the Diocese of Harrisburg, Pennsylvania, with a master's degree in journalism from the University of Missouri and a master's in theology from St. Charles Seminary in Philadelphia.

Introduction

By Very Rev. Peter M. J. Stravinskas, Ph.D., S.T.D.

Fifteen years ago, the planning for *The Catholic Answer* began. All the discussions found all the participants clear about one thing for the new periodical: It had to be committed in a unique way to what was then the newly rediscovered apostolate of apologetics. We have tried to keep that focus sharp over the years.

When people outside the visible boundaries of the Catholic Church raise questions or problems about our teachings, not infrequently topics of a Marian nature surface. And, one must sadly admit that inadequately catechized Catholics often enough have some of the same difficulties. Needless to say, articles on various aspects of Marian doctrine and devotion have been featured throughout the life of *The Catholic Answer*. These pieces have been very popular and, we are told, Catholics and non-Catholics alike have found them very helpful.

What has been surprising to me, in surveying back issues of the magazine, is just how often an article on Our Lady has appeared and how the entire gamut of topics has been covered in her regard. This led to the conclusion that an anthology of our Marian reflections could be valuable. Sometimes our "separated brethren" express amazement at all this attention given to Mary by Catholics, but that is only because they fail to appreciate how intimately connected that woman was to the mystery of the Incarnation and to her divine Son's ongoing work of Redemption. I am, however, particularly pleased at the number of non-Catholic contributors whose thoughts in this formerly "neuralgic" area we have been privileged to publish because that gives us reason to hope that, like any good mother, Our Lady ultimately will be a source of unity for all who profess faith in her Son.

One person who has emphasized the indispensable role played by the Blessed Mother in the economy of salvation is Pope John Paul II. From his first appearance on the balcony of

St. Peter's after his election as Sovereign Pontiff when he declared himself *Totus tuus* ("All yours") to his heavenly Mother, this "Marian" Pope has aided the whole People of God in plumbing the depths of what Pope Paul VI initiated by proclaiming Our Lady as "Mother of the Church" at the closing of the third session of the Second Vatican Council. Indeed, in John Paul's very first encyclical, *Redemptor Hominis* ("Redeemer of Man"), he connected in a powerful way the mission of Christ and the intercession of His Mother for the salvation of the Church and the world: ". . . I implore Mary, the heavenly Mother of the Church, to be so good as to devote herself to this prayer of humanity's new advent, together with us who make up the Church, that is to say, the Mystical Body of her only Son. I hope that through this prayer we will be able to receive the Holy Spirit coming upon us and thus become Christ's witnesses 'to the ends of the earth,' like those who went out from the Upper Room of Jerusalem on the day of Pentecost."

The Holy Father has seen in Mary's life and witness an example for every member of the Church: priests, seminarians, and religious; parents and families; young people; women; the marginalized; the infirm and the oppressed; evangelists and teachers. He sees what the Church has always seen: Mary leads us to Christ. That is the hope that inspires this present volume. As Pope John Paul prepared the Church for the new millennium, he penned some lines that have a special relevance for readers who are embarking on this study of Mary's place in the life of the Church: "I entrust this responsibility of the whole Church to the maternal intercession of Mary, Mother of the Redeemer. She, the mother of fairest love, will be for Christians on the way to the Great Jubilee of the third millennium the star which safely guides their steps to the Lord. May the unassuming young woman of Nazareth, who two thousand years ago offered to the world the Incarnate Word, lead the men and women of the new millennium toward the One Who is 'the true light that enlightens every man.' "

Our Lady, Seat of Wisdom, pray for us.

PART 1

Life of Mary

CHAPTER 1

What Mary's Immaculate Conception Means to Us

By Rev. Peter John Cameron, O.P.

A basic misunderstanding that commonly confronts those being introduced to the mysteries of the faith is one that pertains to the nature of the doctrine of the Immaculate Conception. Does the Immaculate Conception refer to the conception of Mary in her own mother's womb, or to the conception of Jesus in the womb of Mary?

On December 8 the Church answers that question. It honors the conception of Mary in her mother's womb. This Catholic belief has been defined in the following words: "The Most Holy Virgin Mary was, in the first moment of her conception, by a unique gift of grace and privilege of almighty God, in view of the merits of Jesus Christ, the redeemer of mankind, preserved free from all stain of original sin."

However, a sure connection remains between Mary's Immaculate Conception and the conception by the Holy Spirit of Jesus in the womb of Mary, for the Church teaches that the ultimate purpose of the Immaculate Conception of Mary is her motherhood of God. Our approach to this mystery is one way to respond in faith to the Holy Father's intention for the Marian year, namely, that it be a time devoted to studying and promoting the truths surrounding the life of Mary in the mystery of Christ and of the Church (see *Redemptoris Mater,* No. 48).

The mystery of the Immaculate Conception is so fundamental that we gain particular insight into it by returning to the very beginning — to the Garden of Eden. The early Fathers of the Church recognized a number of parallels between Eve and Mary. They commented that the knot of sinfulness produced by Eve's disobedience was untied only by Mary's obedience. The death that came through Eve was reversed in the life that comes through Mary, the Immaculate Conception. The mystery of the Immaculate Conception, then, directly addresses that dilemma that embroils all of humanity universally: the problem of sin.

The confusion over the meaning of the feast is caused in part by a certain ambiguity regarding the term "conception." We commonly understand this word in two ways. We speak of "conceptions" to refer to "ideas" or things that we perceive with our senses. I have my "conception" of the perfect hot-fudge sundae, which may differ drastically from yours. On the other hand, we also speak of "conception" to refer to that principle of fertile, fruitful generation: the conception of a child in the womb of the mother.

Both senses of conception are pivotal in salvation history. The paradise of innocence once enjoyed by Adam and Eve was suddenly shattered by the introduction of something new: a seductive concept! It went something like this: "God is afraid that if you eat from the forbidden tree you will be equal to Him. That is why He said that if you eat from it, you will die." Adam and Eve accepted this perverted "conception," which in turn gained great mastery in controlling and deforming their lives. They exchanged their relationship with God for the profoundly sinful desire *to be God themselves*. At that moment, they surrendered themselves to a conception that was sterile, untrue, and capable of producing only death.

However, God indulges in a bit of divine irony when, in the Immaculate Conception, he preserves Mary from the original sin that is itself the result of identification with that other spurious "conception." Her conception has nothing to do with erroneous ideas about God. In the Immaculate Conception, God reveals to the world how He Himself conceives of His perfect goodness as it is revealed miraculously in the flesh and blood of one specially chosen human creature. And because that conception is manifested in a woman destined to become the Mother of God, we know that God's conception of Himself is meant to be the conception that governs and conforms our life, as it is given to us through Mary's maternal mediation.

Mary, the woman conceived without sin, is the unspotted image of God, His first and most perfect masterpiece in all creation. In order to know the graciousness of God Incarnate, we are required to live united in that one Immaculate Conception, who alone enables Jesus Christ to be known as He deserves to be known.

In Mary's Immaculate Conception, God offers to us two things that were lost by the sin of Adam and Eve. First, the sacredness of human dignity is restored in an irrevocable way in Mary. Within that restoration is borne the definition of true human freedom, which is the fruit of childlike reliance on God. The sin of Adam and Eve led them to desire a perfection that rejected God's offer of sanctity and beatitude from within the human, creaturely condition. By so doing they became, in effect, "immaculate deceptions," filled with a destructive self-love by which they sought to rely only on themselves and on their false conceptions of perfection.

Mary's Immaculate Conception is God's way of giving us a proper and sanctifying way to rely on the sacredness of human personal existence in order to be drawn more closely to Himself. When we rely on the goodness of God as it is miraculously revealed in the Immaculate Conception, we profess that we are unwilling to trust in our own conceptions of goodness and righteousness (a constant temptation). We rely on the sacraments, the Church, the human body and soul of Jesus, and participate in the very holiness of God by relying on the Mother of God. In that mystical union we discover our true dignity and independence because we become truly free of deception and eminently disposed to perfection. The offer of perfect sanctity as well as the redefinition of human worth and dignity was accomplished by God for us at the conception of Mary. How powerfully the Immaculate Conception must defy those who are seduced by the serpent in questioning and attacking the inviolable value of life in the womb.

The original relationship with God that was damaged by enslavement to a sinful conception is restored by our union in the Immaculate Conception, where God manifests Himself ultimately in the birth of Jesus. In their sinful desire to become God, Adam and Eve rejected the divine offer of a living, personal relationship with Him. This remains the outstanding ill effect of a human life lived outside of Mary's Immaculate Conception.

Without the relationship we share with God in Mary, we are driven farther and farther away from Eden by our own self-seeking, imperfect conceptions. This is strongly confirmed by St. Louis-Marie de Montfort when he writes: "I do not believe that any person can achieve intimate union with Our Lord and perfect fidelity to the Holy Spirit, unless he establishes a very deep union with the Blessed Virgin and a great dependence on her help. *It is Mary alone who has found grace before God without the aid of another mere creature.* All others who have found grace with God have done so only through her" (*True Devotion to the Blessed Virgin* [Langley Bucks, England: St. Paul Publications, 1962]; my emphasis).

As we remain united with Mary, we have no reason to fear the selfishness that would draw us into ourselves and away from the offer of God's love. We are no longer tempted to claim God's divinity for ourselves, for He extends the fullness of His perfection to us in Mary's Immaculate Conception. Our unsurpassed joy is to delight in the relationship that invitation makes possible.

Human beings rely on conceptions both to begin and to sustain life, and this same truth applies to the life of faith. The holy season of Advent, then, presents us with a challenge. We can live by our own self-made conceptions, which keep us trapped in our patterns of sin and lead us to death. Or we can live in Mary the Immaculate Conception, the principle of God's ultimate revelation of graciousness and love, by whom we know and share in the life Who is Jesus. As we come to live more deeply united in the mystery of the Immaculate Conception, we can rejoice with an even greater joy as we see the life of Jesus born anew in us who are privileged to share in the very graciousness offered by God to Mary.

CHAPTER 2

At the Annunciation, Mary Became Our Mother Too

By Rev. Romanus Cessario, O.P.

The Incarnation of the Son of God requires that we discover God's purposes in the Word made flesh, revealing God's compassion for sinners. As the angel said to Joseph, "She [Mary] will bear a son, and you shall call his name Jesus, for he will save his people from their sins" (Mt 1:21). At the Annunciation (celebrated on March 25), Mary learned that her motherhood would extend to all those who stand in need of God's mercy and forgiveness. If we reflect on the truth that God chose to come among us as a little Child, we will begin to comprehend what Mary's spiritual motherhood means for the Church.

Why did God choose to come among us as a newborn Baby? One spiritual tradition in the Church tells us that Christ "sends ahead His infancy as an ambassador of peace to reconcile the guilty." In other words, God wants us to know ahead of time that our sins offer no obstacle to His loving us. The same tradition resumes: "When Christ manifested Himself to mortals, He appeared as a Child, a little One more lovable than terrible. Because He came to save and not to judge, He preferred ways of inciting love to means of striking terror." And this "little One" Mary gives to the world. When we willingly surrender to the mystery of the divine childhood, then do we really discover how the Annunciation inaugurates the reign of grace into the world.

In other words, the Incarnation really changes things. In one of his talks on Our Lady, Pope John Paul II clarifies the basis for this claim. "The *fiat* of the Annunciation inaugurates the New Covenant between God and the creature: While it incorporates Jesus into our race according to nature, it incorporates Mary into Him according to grace. The bond between

God and humankind that was broken by sin is now happily restored." But this change occurs only because of what God has accomplished in Jesus and Mary.

The Annunciation celebrates the beginnings of our Christian faith. And even at the inauguration of our salvation, the divine plan involves the Virgin Mary in our sanctification. The angel Gabriel makes this clear in three statements that he addresses to the Blessed Virgin: "The Lord [the Father] is with you" (Lk 1:28); "You will conceive . . . and bear . . . the Son of the Most High" (Lk 1:31-32); "The Holy Spirit will come upon you" (Lk 1:35). The Annunciation discloses the inner vitality of the Triune God.

Indeed, the divine strategy includes Mary. As the Mother of the Messiah, Mary retains a specific responsibility in our spiritual development. By giving us Mary as our mother in the order of salvation, God provides us with a remedy against our reluctance to live in the truth about our own misery. Why? The Holy Father again exclaims: "In Mary every perfection of the creature preexists, and in a manner unspeakably more perfect than in everything else, short of God Himself and the Word made flesh." This means that every sin and imperfection that would otherwise separate us from God finds its remedy in Mary. Of course, that does not mean that Mary supplants our Savior. Since her dignity remains founded on being the Mother of God, everything that she accomplishes for us comes from Christ Himself.

Mary, however, does furnish what we need to escape the vicious blackmail of Satan. "I will put enmity between you and the woman, and between your seed and her seed" (Gn 3:15). To put it differently, there exists in each person a more or less explicit conviction that what we are in ourselves remains unacceptable to God. Still the saints counsel us: "Do not be uneasy because you have sinned grievously." Mary's maternal mediation consists in liberating us from all false fear about sin. She does this because in her, our immaculate mother, we can find the rectitude that we otherwise lack. Rightly do the saints acclaim Mary as the dawn that scatters the darkness of our spiritual isolation.

In another encyclical, *Reconciliatio et Paenitentia* ("Reconciliation and Penance"), the Holy Father establishes the grounds for this hope: "When we realize that God's love for us does not cease in the face of our sin or recoil before our offenses, but becomes even more attentive and generous, then we exclaim in gratitude 'Yes, the Lord is rich in mercy,' and even: 'The Lord is mercy' " (No. 22). Indeed, the saints make compunction a way of life. "Sorrow for sin," wrote St. Teresa of Ávila, "increases in proportion to the divine grace received, and I believe will never quit us until we come to the land where nothing can grieve us any more." The Christian faithful hail Mary as the mother of this sort of divine mercy.

Still, accepting the honest fact of our misery outside of Jesus remains an obstacle for many of us who nonetheless desire to live a good life. Consider, for example, the number of people who have avoided the sacrament of penance for a long time rather than take an honest account of their lives. At the Annunciation, Mary received the news of her unique mission in the Church. "And the angel said to her, 'Do not be afraid, Mary, for you have found favor with God' " (Lk 1:30). The Church remains a continuous movement toward its own center, which is already full reality. Mary herself announces this to our age when she proclaimed at Lourdes: "I am the Immaculate Conception!" Indeed, those who live in Mary, those who repeat her name along with that of her divine Son, discover in themselves the fulfillment of the prophets' saying that a great reconciliation takes place in Christ. Indeed, the Blessed Virgin herself urges us toward this grace of reconciliation.

Finally, the sacrament of penance itself marks an important moment in our return to the center of the Church. Through this sacrament, the Church provides for the need that we experience to hear Jesus Himself speak the words of forgiveness and acceptance. And the Church still asks that we frequently celebrate this sacrament. In fact, among the most appropriate

Lenten penances remains an honest confession. But we should not seek to approach the sacrament of penance without first asking for the grace to live the truth that Jesus gives to us in Mary. For as a Church Father puts it, "The divine Spirit, the love itself of the Father and the Son, came corporally into Mary, and enriching her with graces above all creatures, reposed in her and made her His Spouse, the Queen of heaven and earth." And although a queen, Mary still serves as a real mother in the spiritual order for all those who seek the benefits that derive from the Incarnation.

CHAPTER 3
Mary at Nazareth and Calvary

By Rev. Romanus Cessario, O.P.

When the eternal Son became man in the womb of the Blessed Virgin Mary, God fully manifested His plan of salvation to us. The Annunciation, which took place in "a city of Galilee named Nazareth" (Lk 1:26), celebrates the central event in the history of the world. Our Holy Father describes the significance of this event in his encyclical *Redemptoris Mater* ("Mother of the Redeemer"): "In the salvific design of the Blessed Trinity, the mystery of the Incarnation constitutes the *superabundant* fulfillment of the promise made by God to us after original sin."

The Annunciation — observed on March 25, as mentioned elsewhere — celebrates the day the angel Gabriel told the Blessed Virgin Mary that this promise was a Son, conceived in her by the power of the Holy Spirit. Since March 25 ordinarily falls just before Easter, the Church commemorates the Annunciation shortly before it celebrates Good Friday. At the Annunciation, we behold the revelation of the mystery of the Incarnation at the very beginning of its fulfillment on earth. During Holy Week, and on Good Friday in particular, we celebrate this mystery at the very end of its fulfillment on earth.

Is it not something of a liturgical oddity that Good Friday should come only a few weeks after the Annunciation? St. Thomas Aquinas would not hesitate to reply, "By no means." Why? Aquinas teaches that the Scriptures suggest no other motive for the Incarnation than the forgiveness of our sins. The fifteenth-century Flemish painter Robert Campin depicts this Thomistic truth when he captures the moment of the Incarnation by showing the embryonic Christ advancing toward the Blessed Virgin already carrying His Cross.

At the Annunciation, we learn that the Blessed Virgin Mary stands at the very center of the struggle that accompanies the history of mankind; more particularly, of the struggles that mark the salvation history of each member of the Church. For it is Mary who gives birth to the Son — the "offspring" — Who is at "enmity" with the serpent (see Gn 3:15).

On March 25, then, we join Mary in her private chamber at Nazareth, and rejoice at her conformity to the divine will, with the result that the beginning of the Church occurs within her womb. In a few weeks, we stand by Mary on Mount Calvary near Jerusalem, joining ourselves to her participation in the sacrifice of the blessed fruit of her womb, when Jesus says to the Father, "Yet not what I will, but what thou wilt" (Mk 14:36).

On March 25 we celebrate a marriage feast. In the mystery of the Incarnation, God establishes an indissoluble bond of grace between Himself and His People. Mary is hailed "full of grace" because she is the first person to benefit from this bestowal of divine goodness, the first to become an adopted child of God. In a few weeks, we mourn the death of the Bridegroom, Who "was wounded for our transgressions, . . . bruised for our iniquities" (Is 53:5). In the mystery of the Passion, God perfects His People who are washed clean in the blood of His Son. On March 25 we salute Mary, in the words Dante, in his *Divine Comedy*, places on the lips of St. Bernard, as the "daughter of your Son." Shortly, we invoke Mary as the Sorrowful Mother who before all others experiences the meaning of Jesus' words, "My soul is very sorrowful, even to death" (Mk 14:34). For by the Cross, Mary first beholds the mystery of our redemption, as the Letter to the Hebrews expresses it: "When Christ came into the world, he said, 'Sacrifices and offerings thou hast not desired, but a body hast thou prepared for me; in burnt offerings and sin offerings thou hast taken no pleasure. Then I said, "Lo, I have come to do thy will, O God" ' " (Heb 10:5-7).

Both the Annunciation and Good Friday unite us to the mystery that is Christ. On March 25, we rejoice to know that God unites Himself to our race, such that from the moment of

Mary's *fiat* to the end of time, God's goodness prevails over every form of human iniquity and weakness. During Holy Week, we grieve to discover at what price so great a grace is won. How can we reconcile these two facets of our salvation? How can we both rejoice and grieve at the same time? Let Pope John Paul again lead us to discover the answer: "Before God and before the whole of humanity, Mary remains the unchangeable and inviolable sign of God's election. This election is more powerful than any experience of evil and sin, than all that 'enmity' which marks human history. In this history, Mary remains a sure sign of hope" (*Redemptoris Mater*, No. 11).

Catholics cherish their devotion to Our Lady. Each day, we should hail Mary: Mother of Christ, Mother of our Creator, Mother of our Redeemer, pray for us. Hail, Mary, Vessel of Honor, Singular Vessel of Devotion, House of Gold, pray for us.

CHAPTER 4
Mary's Assumption

By Rev. Richard Sterling Bradford

(Editor's note: The following is a sermon preached by Father Bradford on the Feast of the Assumption of the Blessed Virgin Mary, August 15, 1998, at the Congregation of Saint Athanasius, an Anglican Use parish, in Brookline, Massachusetts. Anglican Use parishes fall under a pastoral provision granted by the Holy See in 1980 for those who were formerly priests and laypeople in the Episcopal Church and wished to enter the Roman Catholic Church. The pastoral provision allows former Episcopalians to celebrate a liturgy from the Vatican-approved Book of Divine Worship, which incorporates certain elements of the Anglican liturgical tradition.)

"He went down with them and came to Nazareth, and was obedient to them" (Lk 2:51).

Today is the day the Catholic Church commemorates the happy death and reception into heaven of the most illustrious of all God's creatures — the Blessed Virgin Mary.

Devotion to Mary springs naturally and inevitably from a true and living faith in Jesus Christ, the Incarnate God, God in the flesh, God made man. Because we worship and adore Jesus, we build beautiful churches to house His sacramental presence. We even honor things associated with Him. A mere sliver of a relic of the True Cross or the shroud that covered His crucified body inspires the most beautiful shrine. Pilgrims come from far and wide to venerate these things in honor of Him. Wherever His presence is, we view that place as consecrated ground.

On this feast of the Assumption, let us think of the Blessed Virgin Mary that way, as a place where His presence has been inextricably and is forever linked, and therefore to be venerated in honor of Him.

The first thirty years of Jesus' life, with the exception of three days, are summed up in these words, "He was subject unto them" (see Lk 2:51). And through all that time Mary was the minister of the will of God to His Son. She taught Him His first prayers; it was she who first explained from the Scriptures to God Incarnate the things concerning Himself. She was the only one who both saw Him born and saw Him die, heard His first baby cry and His last dying words. She shared His passion as no one else. For when one apostle betrayed Jesus and another denied Him, and when all had fled, when His relatives were ashamed of Him and disowned Him, when He was surrounded by a cruel and vindictive mob, then she was there at His side. Mary walked His bloodstained footsteps along the Way of Sorrows. On the Cross it is her blood He sheds. Think about that. It came from no other.

So where does this leave the Blessed Virgin Mary when her life on earth came to a close? In heaven — right away! As she was the closest sharer of His life and sorrows on earth, so she is the closest partaker of His joys.

Jesus taught, and so did the apostles, that all places are not the same in heaven. One star differeth from another star in glory; to one is given command over five, another over ten cities. There is both a left hand and a right hand of the throne. The apostles are to sit on thrones. But Holy Church, brought into all truth by the Holy Spirit, as the Lord promised, teaches that the highest place of all goes to Mary, and God the Father, the Son, and the Holy Ghost welcomed her immediately and bodily as the one creature who corresponded more perfectly than any other to the will and purpose of God. The ascended Lord Jesus, reigning in heaven as Son of God, at the right hand of the Father, ever since this woman's *fiat mihi*, is also Son of Mary, in heaven, always. Mary's baby boy is the Second Person of the Holy Trinity.

Our Lord has taught that He will welcome the saints into heaven saying, "Well done, good and faithful servant; . . . enter into the joy of your master" (Mt 25:21). The saints are the brethren of Jesus by adoption and grace. But Mary is His Mother by nature. They have affinity with Jesus. But she had both affinity and consanguinity.

The New Testament does not mention the Assumption of Mary. But the New Testament is not about Mary; it is about her Son. That is the way she would have it. But we would be very faithless if we doubted that Our Lady is glorified with her Son, and that she is praying for us that we also may know, as she does, the final fruits of faithfulness, and reign with Christ in glory.

Nothing ever gets between Mary and her Son. She is devoted to those who love, honor, worship, obey, and adore Him. For them she is the most powerful intercessor ever and always. Her assumption into heaven encourages us to say: "Holy Mary, pray for us."

CHAPTER 5
The Imitation of Mary

By Dave Armstrong

Many Christians have trouble identifying with the Blessed Virgin Mary because of her sinlessness and Immaculate Conception, and feel that the extraordinary graces given to Mary make it impossible for the rest of us to emulate or imitate her.

Closely related to this opinion is the thought that it would have been more profound if God had chosen a "normal" woman through whom to enter the world. And these notions lend themselves toward skepticism about the Immaculate Conception and other Marian beliefs held by Catholics, Orthodox, and even some traditional Protestants.

This is a worthy, honest question to consider, and deserves a solid Catholic response. Miserable sinners like us indeed find themselves in a very awkward position in relationship to God and the perfect Blessed Virgin Mary. The Catholic, nevertheless, can sensibly and biblically respond to this perceived problem from several different angles.

First, we need to distinguish between relating to Mary and emulating her. Since she was indeed without sin (both original and actual), in that sense it is difficult to "walk in her shoes." Yet, with regard to imitation, it is a fact of life that in our better moments we all strive to emulate people who are "superior" to us, whom we admire and look up to — those who have succeeded in areas we still yearn for and dream about. That's what all the talk about "role models" is about. If we didn't have a high goal to strive for, how could we improve and become the type of people we want to be?

Second, I think what Catholics have most revered about Mary through the centuries is her humility and willingness to be mightily used by God as the *Theotokos* ("God-bearer"). In this sense she is like us: a mere human being who said "yes" to God, thus reversing the "no" of Eve (hence her designation as the "Second Eve" by the Fathers of the Church). This is the Mary of the Annunciation (see Lk 1:38, 48).

Now, one might counter with the objection that she "had" to say yes, being sinless, yet Catholics would not hold to that assertion, since we also believe in free will. It is true of all of us that we must agree to accept and cooperate with the graces that always originate from God (see 1 Cor 3:8-9, 15:10; 2 Cor 6:1). We are, in a sense, "co-laborers" with God. We do not adhere to fatalism or determinism (even Calvinists deny that they hold such a view). If we take the logic that she "had" to do it (that, therefore, it wasn't meritorious), taking it to its logical conclusion, we would also have to say that God's voluntary good actions are not good, since He is unable — by the nature of things — to sin. So we assert that Mary did the right thing, and that she was a created human being like the rest of us, even though without sin, and that this is both her glory and her commonality with us.

Third, Mary is not intrinsically superior, in essence, to the rest of us. She received from God all of the grace that she possessed in abundance (see Lk 1:28; "full of grace" in some translations, including the *Revised Standard Version*). She was merely given more of it at one time, and earlier, than we. All human beings who are to be saved for eternity in heaven will one day be without sin, unstained, immaculate, just as Mary was from conception, and just as all of us were meant to be, but for the Fall of Adam and Eve. That's why Cardinal John Henry Newman said it was easier to believe in the Immaculate Conception than it was to accept the fact that all human beings are conceived in original sin, since it was one mere exception to the universal rule.

Fourth, while it is appealing to ponder a sinful Mary whom God could have used, as well (which is indeed not an impossible hypothetical scenario — and one I used to argue also), God chose, rather, to make her sinless, since this was appropriate for the "ark of the new covenant" who carried God Incarnate and shared even her own blood with Him *in utero*. So

God chose to act in a special way to preserve Mary from sin.

It doesn't seem unreasonable at all to believe that He would do that, given that He will eventually cleanse totally all saved persons so that they will be fit for heaven. If we must be clean to enter heaven and stand in God's presence (see Rev 21:27), then it seems only proper for the Mother of God to possess a commensurate righteousness for that unfathomable task, privilege, and honor. In fact, if I were she, I would much rather have been granted that special grace than to have to face that awesome situation as a sinner.

Fifth, there are plenty of other sinful, "weak" models in Scripture that we can relate to as like us — vacillating, over-zealous Peter; perhaps proud, tempestuous Paul; stuttering Moses and his wimpy brother Aaron; blame-shifting Adam; murderous and adulterous David; doubting Thomas; deceptive Jacob; sexually weak Samson; drunken, incestuous Noah, etc. I don't think it is implausible for God to spare one lone human being (His earthly Mother at that) from the onslaught of original sin. In fact, I wonder myself why He didn't make more people sinless.

Finally, getting back to the first point, I think this objection fails in the final analysis because it is unscriptural. We are commanded to imitate the apostle Paul and other saints (see 1 Cor 4:16; Phil 3:17; 2 Thes 3:7-9; Heb 6:12; Jas 5:10-11), which is difficult enough. St. Paul sinned as we do, but he also did extraordinary things that in all likelihood we will never accomplish. He was an apostle. Yet we are called to "imitate" him.

Christianity is filled with this sort of striving for what in fact is virtually unattainable in this lifetime. That's one of the many paradoxes of our faith. We may not achieve a 100 percent grade, but we can shoot for a 90, or 80 (speaking of sanctification, not the grounds of salvation — Catholics are not Pelagians who believe in salvation by man-originated works), as God allows, and as we are faithful in allowing Him to do His work in us. The ideals are always there to shoot for.

Now, the rub is that St. Paul, in turn, imitates Christ, and calls us to do that as well (see 1 Cor 11:1; 1 Thes 1:6). Here we are in the same boat as with Mary, and much more so, since this is God Incarnate. Obviously, we will not be able to "imitate" Him perfectly, but we are called to do our best, and live by His example. And in Our Lord Jesus we find the same humility (of course, even more profound) that we find in Mary: He humbled Himself first by giving up divine prerogatives and becoming man (see Phil 2:5-7) and then dying on the Cross (see Phil 2:8). And that is the glory of the Incarnation itself, the fact that God would so humble Himself out of love for us as to become one of us — like His own creatures. C. S. Lewis compared that act to a person becoming an ant. We don't say that we can't relate to Christ because He is God, but that we can relate to Him, since He is a man: "For we have not a high priest who is unable to sympathize with our weaknesses, but one who in every respect has been tempted as we are, yet without sinning" (Heb 4:15; see also 4:16; 5:7-8; 2:17-18; Is 53:3; 2 Cor 5:21; 1 Pt 2:19-21).

Therefore, since we are expressly informed in Scripture that Jesus, Our Lord and God, Who did not and could not sin, can nevertheless relate to us, "sympathize with our weaknesses," and has been tested like us "in every respect," we can relate all the more so to Mary, who is a creature as we are, yet without sin.

In other words, it is not sinlessness that is inherently opposed to human nature, as if sin and concupiscence were the "normal" state. Rather, it is sin that is "unhuman," since it stands in the way of what God intended for the human race, and what will one day indeed be accomplished among the saved and the elect. Thus the Blessed Virgin Mary is more "human" than all of us, and therefore can help us (by example and intercession) to be what we should be: more like Jesus, her beloved Son, and less bound to sin. She is the example of what all of us can be more like in this life, and what we assuredly will essentially be in the next if we persevere in the faith.

Catholic Christianity recognizes and venerates Our Lady, the Perpetual Virgin and Immaculate Mother of God, as the exemplar of what redeemed humanity will one day be: the forerunner, the quintessential Christian and symbol of the Church itself, our spiritual mother and Queen of Heaven, who was spared by God's grace the curse of death and immediately received her glorious resurrected body after her earthly sojourn had come to an end. And that's why we and others have fulfilled the prophecy that Mary gave concerning herself: "Henceforth all generations will call me blessed" (Lk 1:48).

And why is she blessed?

"For he who is mighty has done great things for me, and holy is his name" (Lk 1:49).

Mary is always glorifying God the Father and Jesus, never herself, for this is her purpose and calling. All of the Marian doctrines are Christocentric. They were promulgated in the first place so that Jesus Christ would be glorified, not Mary. And this is why Catholics have venerated her above all creatures, and why any Christian can indeed "relate to" and "identify with" her, because she glorifies and imitates God, and that is what all serious Christians want to do (and are commanded to do) too.

PART 2

Doctrine

CHAPTER 6
A Marian Tapestry: Mary in the New Catechism

By Sister Marianne Lorraine Trouvé, F.S.P.

Fighting the crowds, I made my way through Grand Central Station in New York. Suddenly, I felt a tug and realized someone had reached out for the rosary hanging at the side of my habit. I turned and saw a "bag lady" kissing it. That simple gesture of faith reminded me that we have a mother in heaven who looks after us, no matter how poor or abandoned we may be.

Devotion to Mary is deeply rooted in the Catholic tradition. Well-informed Catholics know the difference between the Immaculate Conception and the Virgin Birth, and that Mary is the Mother of God and was assumed into heaven. But each of those teachings is not an isolated fact. They're more like the pieces of a jigsaw puzzle that need to be seen together, joined to all the other pieces to form a picture of a waterfall, a forest, or a mountain. The *Catechism of the Catholic Church* presents its teaching on Mary in such a way that it helps us see it as a harmonious unity, like a beautifully woven tapestry.

The *Catechism* draws the various strands of doctrine together and presents the best of recent developments in Marian theology. It is interesting to compare how the Roman Catechism — the official catechism that was put out after the Council of Trent (1545-1563) — differs from the new *Catechism* in its treatment of Mary. The Roman Catechism is rather sketchy, mentioning Mary only in discussing the article of the Creed in which it is stated that Christ was "born of the Virgin Mary." A later section also has two paragraphs on Marian prayer.

In contrast, the new *Catechism*'s treatment of Mary is quite extensive, falling into three main sections, plus a brief section on Mary's prayer: Mary in relation to Christ (Nos. 487-507); Mary in relation to the Holy Spirit (Nos. 721-726); Mary in relation to the Church (Nos. 963-972); the prayer of Mary (Nos. 2617-2619, 2673-2679).

But the *Catechism*'s discussion of Mary is not limited to these articles. References to her are sprinkled throughout the text. It seems that the Church wants us to see Mary in relation to every aspect of Catholic life. Within this context, two themes stand out: Mary's role in the plan of salvation, and Mary as a model of holiness.

Mary's Role in the Plan of Salvation

Marian theology has greatly developed recently in the Church, becoming more clearly situated in the context of Christology. The *Catechism* states: "What the Catholic faith believes about Mary is based on what it believes about Christ, and what it teaches about Mary illumines in turn its faith in Christ" (No. 487).

Right from the beginning of its treatment of Mary, the *Catechism* spotlights Jesus Christ, for Mary is important only in relation to Jesus. From the earliest centuries, what the Church taught about Mary derived from what it taught about Christ. For example, in the year 431, the Council of Ephesus declared Mary truly to be the Mother of God, against Nestorius, who denied it. But Nestorius's basic error was about Christ. By proclaiming Mary's divine motherhood, the Church was actually safeguarding the truth about the divinity of Christ.

The *Catechism* also brings out that Mary's role must be understood in relation to the Church. This emphasis has better focused Marian teaching in the light of salvation history.

In the first Marian section in the *Catechism* (Nos. 487-511) found in Part One, the *Catechism* discusses four main points: (1) Mary's predestination; (2) her Immaculate Conception; (3) her divine motherhood; and (4) her virginity. It weaves the themes together like a loom spinning cloth.

God chose Mary to be the Mother of His Son. He wanted to invite a human being to cooperate freely in the plan of salvation. God gave Mary special gifts of grace in view of her unique mission. It would not have been fitting for the Mother of God to have had any stain of sin; so, through Mary's Immaculate Conception, God preserved her from original sin. Alone of all human persons, she entered this world enriched with grace. This privilege was given in view of her role in the plan of salvation. She was redeemed by Christ in a more abundant way so that she would be fully prepared to be God's Mother. "In order for Mary to be able to give the free assent of her faith to the announcement of her vocation, it was necessary that she be wholly borne by God's grace" (No. 490).

Mary's role as the Mother of God is her key position in salvation history. Everything about her revolves around that. Mary was privileged to bring the Son of God into the world. He took on flesh and blood through her. "The One whom she conceived as man by the Holy Spirit, who truly became her Son according to the flesh, was none other than the Father's eternal Son, the second person of the Holy Trinity. Hence the Church confesses that Mary is truly 'Mother of God' " (No. 495).

The fact that she is the Mother of God also explains Mary's virginity. The *Catechism* points out that her "virginity manifests God's absolute initiative in the Incarnation. Jesus has only God as Father" (No. 503). After Jesus' birth, Mary remained a virgin for the rest of her life, as a *"sign of her faith . . .* , and of her undivided gift of herself to God's will" (No. 506; emphasis in original).

Mary also has a special relation to the Holy Spirit, Who prepared her for her role through special gifts of grace. Luke notes that the Spirit overshadowed Mary at the Annunciation (see Lk 1:35). Because she gave birth to the Son of God, Mary made God visible. Through her, the Holy Spirit manifested the Father's Son to the world. The *Catechism* beautifully states that Mary "is the burning bush of the definitive theophany" (No. 724).

The *Catechism* also explains how Mary is closely connected with the Church. After returning to the Father, Jesus sent the Holy Spirit on the Church to continue Jesus' saving mission in the world. On the first Pentecost, the Holy Spirit descended with tongues of fire on the apostles, who were with Mary in the Upper Room. This scene, depicted in the second chapter of the Acts of the Apostles, parallels Luke's description of the Annunciation. Just as Mary received the Holy Spirit and became the Mother of the Redeemer, so as the apostles received the Holy Spirit on Pentecost did she become the Mother of the Church. "She is 'clearly the mother of the members of Christ' . . . , since she has by her charity joined in bringing about the birth of believers in the Church, who are members of its head" (No. 963).

As our mother in the order of grace, "Mary's role in the Church is inseparable from her union with Christ and flows directly from it" (No. 964). Far from diminishing the role of Christ as the one Mediator, Mary's intercession depends entirely on the redemptive work of Jesus.

The *Catechism* also notes that as a virgin and mother, Mary is a symbol of the Church. Through baptism, the Church brings forth new members into God's life. The Church too "is a virgin, who keeps in its entirety and purity the faith she pledged to her spouse" (No. 507).

Mary As a Model of Holiness

The *Catechism* calls Mary an "eschatological icon of the Church" (subhead preceding No. 972). This simply means that we already see in her the beauty of perfect holiness that the Church will finally reach at the end of history. "In her, the Church is already the 'all-holy'" (No. 829). In this light, the doctrine of Mary's assumption clarifies that she has already received that which awaits us at the end of time: the resurrection and glorification of our bodies.

Mary is also a model of faith and charity. Her life shows us how an authentic disciple of the Lord acts. Upon hearing of Elizabeth's pregnancy, Mary hurried to help the older woman through that demanding time. Mary's charity led her to sacrifice herself in practical ways. We can imagine her cooking meals, fetching a jug of water at the village well, and perhaps sewing tiny clothes for the baby. The Gospel portrays her as the humble, silent, and loving follower of Jesus. She never claims the spotlight; rather, she directs everyone to her Son.

The *Catechism*'s section on Mary's prayer highlights how her prayer embodied her total gift of self to God. At the Annunciation, she simply replied, "Behold the servant of the Lord" (see Lk 1:38). She was always ready to do whatever God wanted. " 'Fiat': this is Christian prayer: to be wholly God's, because he is wholly ours" (No. 2617).

Mary teaches us how to pray. As the perfect exemplar of prayer, Mary shows us how to remain in communion with her Son through our prayer. "Our filial prayer unites us in the Church with the Mother of Jesus" (No. 2673). What a striking image this is — to pray together with Mary as members of the Church. It might be more usual to think of ourselves as praying *to* Mary, rather than with her as the *Catechism* suggests. Imagine being present at a prayer meeting with the Blessed Mother — yet in the communion of saints this is a reality.

In a beautiful exposition of the Hail Mary (Nos. 2676-2677), the *Catechism* points out how this prayer embodies a twofold movement: "The first 'magnifies' the Lord for the 'great things' he did for his lowly servant and through her for all human beings; the second entrusts the supplications and praises of the children of God to the Mother of Jesus, because she now knows the humanity which, in her, the Son of God espoused" (No. 2675). This section concludes by noting that "Mary is the perfect *Orans* (pray-er), a figure of the Church. . . . The prayer of the Church is sustained by the prayer of Mary and united with it in hope" (No. 2679).

Mary appears throughout the entire *Catechism* as the first and most faithful disciple of the Lord. She has gone before us on the way of faith, having endured trials and sufferings while on earth. Now in heaven, she intercedes for us who struggle on the way to eternal life. As a mother and helper, she still obtains graces and favors for all those who turn to her in their needs.

CHAPTER 7

Mary's Virginity in Light of Jewish Law and Tradition

By Brother Anthony M. Opisso

From the earliest biblical days, adultery carried with it a sense of defilement, so that a woman who had known contact with another man, even if by force, was considered no longer fit to be visited by her husband (see Gn 49:4; 2 Sm 20:3). The Deuteronomic code teaches that a woman who is divorced by her husband and thereafter marries another man likewise cannot return to her former husband (see Dt 24:1-4).

Not only adultery but even a legitimate marriage renders a woman unfit to be taken by her first husband. As the Lord said through the prophet Jeremiah: "If a man divorces his wife and she goes from him and becomes another man's wife, will he return to her? Would not that land [his wife's body] be greatly polluted?" (Jer 3:1). In rabbinic law, a woman who has committed adultery is "defiled" and cannot remain the wife of her husband, but must be divorced.

Furthermore, any intimate male contact by the wife with Jew or Gentile — potent or impotent, natural or unnatural — makes divorce compulsory.

In Jewish law, a man betrothed to a woman was considered legally married to her. The word for "betrothed" in Hebrew is *Kiddush,* a word that is derived from the Hebrew word *Kadash,* which means "holy," "consecrated," "set apart." By betrothal (as in Mt 1:18; Lk 1:27) or marriage, a woman became the peculiar property of her husband, forbidden to others. The Oral Law of Kiddushin (Marriages and Engagements) states: "The husband prohibits his wife to the whole world like an object which is dedicated to the Sanctuary."

We know from the Gospel of St. Matthew (1:19) that Joseph, the husband of Mary, was "a just man," a devout law-abiding Jew. Having noticed that Mary was pregnant and that he, her betrothed, had nothing to do with the pregnancy, Joseph had either to condemn her publicly and have her put to death for adultery (see Dt 22:22-29) or put her away privately. His decision was made when an angel appeared to him in a dream, saying: "Joseph, son of David, do not fear to take Mary as your wife, for that which is conceived in her is of the Holy Spirit; she will bear a son, and you shall call His name Jesus, for he will save his people from their sins" (Mt 1:20-21). The angel does not use the phrase for marital union, "go in to her" (as in Gn 30:3, 4, 16) or "come together" (as in Mt 1:18); instead, he uses a word that simply means leading her into the house as a wife (*paralambano gunaika*) but not cohabiting with her. For when the angel revealed to him that Mary was truly the spouse of the Holy Spirit, Joseph could take Mary, his betrothed, into his house as a wife, but he could never have intercourse with her because according to the law she was forbidden to him for all time.

We also have to take into consideration that when Mary was told by the archangel Gabriel, "And behold, you will conceive in your womb and bear a son, and you shall call his name Jesus" (Lk 1:31), he also added that this was to come about because, as Luke tells us, "The Holy Spirit will come upon you, and the power of the Most High will overshadow you; therefore the Holy One to be born shall be called the Son of God" (Lk 1:35). By stating it in those terms, the archangel declared to Mary that God would enter into a marital relationship with her, causing her to conceive His Son in her womb. For "to lay one's power [*reshuth*] over a woman" was a euphemism for having a marital relationship with her. Likewise "to overshadow" (as in Lk 1:35) by spreading the "wing" or "cloak" over a woman was another euphemism for having marital relations with her.

Thus, the rabbis commented that Ruth was chaste in her wording when she asked Boaz to have marital relations with her by saying to him: "I am Ruth your handmaid; spread therefore your cloak [literally, "wing": *kanaph*] over your handmaid for you are my next-of-kin" (Ruth 3:9).

Another Aramaic-Hebrew word for "cloak" is *tallith*, and is derived from *tellal*, which means "shadow." Thus, "to spread one's cloak [*tallith*] over a woman" means to cohabit with her. Did not the Lord say to His bride Israel: "I am married to you" (see Jer 3:14) and "your Maker is your husband" (Is 54:5; see also Jer 31:32)? And what is more intimate than what the Lord said to His bride: "You developed, you grew, you came to full womanhood; your breasts became firm and your hair grew . . . you were naked . . . and I saw that you were now old enough for love so I spread my cloak over you . . . I gave you my oath, I entered into a covenant with you and you became mine, says the Lord God" (Ezek 16:7, 8).

Having been enlightened by an angel in a dream regarding her pregnancy, and perhaps being further enlightened by Mary concerning the words of the archangel Gabriel to her at the Annunciation, Joseph knew that God had conducted Himself as a husband in regard to Mary. She was now prohibited to him for all time, and for the sake of the Child and Mary, he could only live with her in an absolutely chaste relationship.

Living a celibate life within marriage was not unknown in Jewish tradition. It was told that Moses, who was married, remained continent the rest of his life after the command to abstain from sexual intercourse (see Ex 19:15) given in preparation for the revelation at Mount Sinai. There was also a tradition that the seventy elders abstained thereafter from their wives after their call, and so did Eldad and Medad when the spirit of the prophecy came upon them; indeed, it was said that the prophets became celibate after the Word of the Lord was communicated to them.

Elijah and Elisha were celibate all their lives. When for the sake of the Torah (that is, intense study in it), a rabbi would abstain from relations with his wife, it was deemed permissible, for he was then cohabiting with the Shekinah (the "Divine Presence") in the Torah.

It is well known that the rabbis spoke concerning the obligation of all males to be married and procreate: "He who abstains from procreation is regarded as though he had shed blood." According to an ancient saying, a man is only half a man without a wife; it cites Genesis, where it is said: "Male and female he [God] created them, and he blessed them and named them Man [or Adam, from the Hebrew *adham*]" (5:2). Nevertheless, "if a person cleaves to the study of the Torah (i.e., dedicates all his time to it) like Simeon ben Azzai, his refusal to marry can be condoned" (Shukhan Arukh, BH 1:4).

Rabbinic scholar Simeon ben Azzai (early second century A.D.) was extraordinary in his learning. It was said of him: "With the passing of Ben Azzai diligent scholars passed from the earth" (Sotah 9:15). He never married and was celibate all his life so as not to be distracted from his studies; because he considered the Torah his wife for whom he always yearned with all his soul, he justified his bachelorhood. He was an outstanding scholar and also renowned for his saintliness.

Jewish tradition also mentions the celibate *Zenu'im* (literally, "chaste ones") to whom the secret of the Name of God was entrusted, for they were able to preserve the Holy Name in "perfect purity." Those in hope of a divine revelation consequently refrained from sexual intercourse and were strict in matters of purity (see Rev 14:2-5). Philo wrote on the celibacy of the Jewish Essenes hundreds of years before the discovery of their settlements in Qumran by the Dead Sea.

Philo Judaeus (c. 20 B.C.-c. A.D. 50), a Jewish philosopher whose works include *De vita contemplativa* and *De Abrahamo*, wrote concerning Jewish women who were "virgins who have kept their chastity not under compulsion, like some Greek priestesses, but of their own free will in their ardent yearning for Wisdom. Eager to have Wisdom for their life-mate, they have spurned the pleasures of the body and desire no mortal offspring but those immortal children which only the soul that is dear to God can bring forth to birth" (Philo, *Cont.* 68; see also *Abr.* 100). For "the chaste are rewarded by receiving illumination from the concealed heavenly light" (Zohar II.229b-230a). Because "if the understanding is safe and unimpaired, free from the oppression of the iniquities or passions . . . it will gaze clearly on all that is worthy of contemplation" (Philo, *Sob.* I.5). Conversely, "the understanding of the pleasure-loving man is blind and unable to see those things that are worth seeing . . . the sight of which is wonderful to behold and desirable" (Philo, *Q. Gen.* IV. 245).

As the recipient of the great revelation that what was conceived in the womb of Mary, his betrothed, was of the Holy Spirit and that the Child to be born was destined to save His people from their sins, surely Joseph knew that he was called to take care of Mary and her Child, the Messiah, for the rest of his life, which is why the angel told him to take Mary as his wife. We may reasonably assume that Mary herself now shared with him all that the archangel Gabriel said to her. No less a Person than "the Son of God" (Lk 1:35) was to be entrusted to his care under the shelter of his humble home, now become the Holy of Holies.

Jewish tradition mentions that although the people had to abstain from sexual relations with their wives for only three days prior to the revelation at Mount Sinai (see Ex 19:15), Moses chose to remain continent the rest of his life with the full approval of God. The rabbis explained that this was so because Moses knew that he was personally appointed to commune with God not only at Mount Sinai but in general throughout the forty years of sojourning in the wilderness. For this reason, Moses kept himself "apart from woman," remaining in the sanctity of separation to be at the beck and call of God at all times, and the rabbis cited God's command to Moses in Deuteronomy 5:28 as evidence.

Again, we may be sure that St. Joseph remained celibate all his life because throughout his married years he was in daily attendance and communication with Jesus: the Incarnate Word of God.

CHAPTER 8
A Difficult, Daring Doctrine: The Immaculate Conception

By Rev. William Weary

The Church Fathers said little about it, the Bible even less. Some saints outright denied it, and the Church long delayed in defining it.

Yet ever since Pope Pius IX infallibly proclaimed the Immaculate Conception of the Blessed Virgin Mary as a dogma, it has been presented as a truth always believed by the Church.

What do we make of all this? Is there any evidence in Scripture and Tradition for this belief that Mary was free from all original and actual sin from the first moment of her existence in her mother's womb?

There is, but first, a full understanding must be obtained of Divine Revelation, the truth revealed to us by God through His Church's Sacred Scripture and Sacred Tradition.

While Catholics (and most Protestants) believe that Revelation ended with the death of the last apostle, Catholics also believe that the Church's understanding of that given Revelation grows, develops, and sharpens over time.

That means that a certain truth — like the Immaculate Conception — can be part of the Church's faith since the beginning but still become more and more clarified in the minds and hearts of the faithful over time. It can be subtle for a while, to become more explicit later.

For instance, many scholars have seen Mary's Immaculate Conception "contained within" the angel's Annunciation greeting to her, "Hail, full of grace" (Luke 1:28). Indeed, the original Greek for "full of grace" does denote an abundance and perfection that is certainly compatible with Church teaching on the Immaculate Conception.

Others have seen the dogma as implied in the "woman clothed with the sun" of Revelation 12:1-6. So while this dogma (a doctrine taught by the Church for all to believe as part of Divine Revelation) is not explicit in the Bible, Catholics believe it is nevertheless implied in such passages.

What about early Church writings? The first evidence comes from St. Ephraem of Syria (c. 306-373), a poet, hymn writer, and deacon. In his Nisibene Hymns he addresses Christ and Mary in this way: "Thou alone and thy mother are in all things fair; for there is no flaw in thee and no stain in thy mother." These and similar passages of Ephraem show at least an emerging belief in the Immaculate Conception.

St. Ambrose (340-397), bishop of Milan, Italy, writes: "Adopt me, however, not from Sarah but from Mary, so that it might be (from) an incorrupt virgin, virgin by grace, free from all stain of sins."

About the same time, St. Augustine of Hippo (354-430) said that sin covered the whole human race "except for the holy Virgin about whom I do not wish any question to be raised when sin is being discussed — for whence do we know what greater grace of complete triumph over sin has been given to her?"

Augustine was only referring here to Mary's freedom from actual sin. Other passages he wrote indicate he believed her to fall under original sin's dominion. In fact, not a few fourth- and fifth-century saints believed that Mary was not only born into original sin but that she committed personal (actual) sins too.

These saints could not see Mary being exempt from sin's universality as spoken by Paul in his Letter to the Romans: "All have sinned and fall short of the glory of God" (3:23). And many, like Augustine, believed (incorrectly) that original sin was passed on through sexual intercourse. Since everyone agreed that Mary was conceived the normal way, she would have inherited Adam's curse like the rest of us, or so went the reasoning.

Others theorized that, although conceived in original sin, Mary was cleansed of it later in her life — perhaps at the Annunciation — but before conceiving Jesus in her womb, in order to be a pure receptacle for the Divine Word made flesh. These theories seemed to their proponents more compatible with Scripture, since they placed Mary at least for a time under sin and thus in need of a Redeemer.

But new feast days on the Eastern Church calendar indicated differing opinions. The first, in sixth-century Syria, was a feast of the Nativity of the Virgin. This was unusual, since only the death dates of saints, especially martyrs, were celebrated, as their "birthday" to eternal life.

The exception to this rule was the Birth of John the Baptist, celebrated because of the common belief that he had been rendered "sanctified," or sinless, when he leapt inside his mother Elizabeth's womb at Mary's Visitation (see Lk 1:41). Was this new feast of Mary's Nativity saying that she too was sinless at birth like the Baptist? It would seem so.

About a hundred years later, a feast appeared celebrating Mary's *conception* in her own mother's womb. No other saint had been so honored before. The ancient records at this time do not speak explicitly of her sinlessness at conception, but the implications are clear, especially in other writings.

For example, St. Sophronius (d. 638), patriarch of Jerusalem, wrote of Mary: "Many saints appeared before thee but none was filled with grace as thou . . . no one has been purified in advance as thou hast been. . . . Thou dost surpass all that is most excellent in man. . . ." That phrase "purified in advance" sounds close to current belief in the Immaculate Conception.

The first to write clearly of Mary's total freedom from all sin from the first moment of her conception was St. John Damascene (690-749). Addressing Mary's father and mother, he writes: "O happy loins of Joachim, which had produced a germ (seed) which is all immaculate. O wondrous womb of Anne in which an all-holy child slowly grew and took shape."

Surprising evidence of early Church belief in Mary's sinlessness comes from Islam, founded in the seventh century, which borrowed much from Christian belief. Islam's scriptures, the Koran, have a passage saying, "Every Adam's son coming into the world is touched by Satan except for Mary's Son and His mother."

But equally surprising opposition to the belief comes from two great saints, Bernard of Clairvaux (1090-1153) and Thomas Aquinas (c. 1225-1274). In a famous letter Bernard — apparently unaware of the Eastern tradition — reprimands the canons of Lyons, France, for celebrating a new feast of Mary's conception in her mother's womb. He objects to implications of the feast that Mary was sinless from conception, despite his otherwise deep Marian devotion. And Aquinas too rejects her Immaculate Conception in his *Summa Theologica* because he thought such a privilege would free her from need for a Redeemer.

Remember that the Church had not officially ruled on the question in their time, so differences of opinion were allowed. And note well that both saints did believe that Mary was rendered sinless while in her mother's womb — but only after her conception.

This apparent problem of Mary's Immaculate Conception removing her from Christ's salvific act was solved by John Duns Scotus (c. 1265-1308), a Scottish Franciscan and theologian. He said that Mary still calls Christ her Savior because she was saved by Him in this way: While the rest of humanity is saved *after* falling into sin, Mary was *prevented* from falling into sin, original or actual, at all.

He said that her freedom from all sin is still a gift given her, flowing from the merits of Christ's death and resurrection, reaching her even before those events took place in time.

Thus, Mary would still fall under Romans 3:23 in a remote way, since she *would have* fallen into sin had not God intervened for her.

Another five hundred years of debate and discussion would follow, until Pius IX would solemnly declare that indeed Mary was "free from all stain of original sin."

Despite this long and winding road, we can say that the truth of Mary's complete sinlessness was always, in some way, preserved in the general Deposit of the Faith. This was confirmed not only by the Pope's 1854 statement but by that of a mysterious lady who appeared four years later to a little peasant girl, Bernadette, in rural France. When asked by Bernadette to identify herself, the Lady would answer by saying, "I am the Immaculate Conception."

CHAPTER 9
Mary's Immaculate Conception

By Rev. Charles Dickson

In 1854, when Pope Pius IX took the bold step of raising belief in the Immaculate Conception of the Blessed Virgin Mary to the status of a formal doctrine in the Church, it was sure to spark controversy. Seen from the perspective of history, it was, at the time, a daring move, which the Pontiff made to signal his determined opposition to the antireligious spirit that was sweeping across Europe at the time.

While it was a bold act, there were those who questioned the pronouncement then, and there are those who continue to question whether or not it was a wise one. Since the mood of the time was already secular and anticlerical, would not the promulgation of new dogma prove to be just another burden for the Church to overcome in its attempt to communicate with the world? And if it might prove to be a burden in relation to the world, might it not also become a barrier between Rome and the other Christian communities as well? How would Eastern Orthodoxy respond? And what about the Anglicans and the many Protestant groups?

Was Pope Pius IX only a reactionary autocrat determined to fight the spirit of his age, or is there a wisdom in the dogma of the Immaculate Conception that transcends the boundaries of the particular age in which it was born?

To be sure, the doctrine Pope Pius IX set forth was not some universally accepted tenet of Christian faith, clearly founded on Scripture and ancient tradition (although some argument may be made on this), and agreed on by all Christians, particularly the great theologians. The Immaculate Conception was a teaching with which even the prince of theologians, St. Thomas Aquinas, had problems. Aquinas did not deny the sanctification of Mary while she was still in the womb of St. Anne before her birth, but he did express some difficulty extending this sanctification back to the first moment of conception. It was more of what one might call a technical question than a denial of the spirit of the teaching for him. It was the type of question with which we continue to struggle today regarding the "moment" (if indeed it can be defined) when a person comes into being. Is it, for example, the moment of union between ovum and spermatozoon or some other moment of what biologists and anthropologists often refer to as "animation"?

For Thomas Aquinas and other theologians, most of the objections to the doctrine lay with those technical questions of biology and anthropology and not with a denial that Mary was sanctified at or near the beginning of her life. While debate continued among Catholic theologians, the Eastern Orthodox theologian Vladimir Lossky stated, "I do not see any irresoluble conflict between the doctrine of the Immaculate Conception and the full humanity and freedom of Mary as of the same race as Eve."

Response from the Anglican community has been less enthusiastic. In the agreed-upon statement regarding "Authority in the Church," produced by the Anglican-Roman Catholic International Commission, we read: "Special difficulties are created by the recent Marian dogmas because Anglicans doubt the appropriateness or even the possibility of defining them as essential to believers."

Somewhat predictably, Protestant critics have been even less supportive. Karl Barth, in his *Church Dogmatics,* had many positive things to say about Mary, but he rejected Mariological dogmas on the basis that he considered them to be arbitrary innovations not justified by Scripture and also that, for him, seemed to contradict the principle of *sola gratia* ("grace alone").

All this has led to the suggestion in some quarters that some Christian doctrines, including those of a Mariological nature, be regarded as inessential, thus allowing for a variety of interpretations of belief. Ludwig Ott's *Fundamentals of Catholic Dogma* admits that the Immaculate Conception is not explicitly taught in Scripture, and he freely acknowledges that neither the Greek nor Latin Fathers teach this doctrine. But he claims it is implicit in their teachings about the holiness and purity of Mary, and in the contrast that the Fathers developed between the figures of Mary and of Eve.

But if the doctrine of the Immaculate Conception is to be recognized as a legitimate item in Christian theology, this will be accomplished by showing that it is implicative of all other Christian truths. It must be shown that Mariological dogma is not a superfluous embellishment but an integral element to our understanding of anthropology, Christology, and soteriology.

The words of the dogma read: "We declare . . . that the most Blessed Virgin Mary in the first moment of her conception was, by the unique grace and privilege of God, in view of the merits of Jesus Christ the Savior of the human race, preserved intact from all stain of original sin."

What is important for understanding the doctrine of the Immaculate Conception is that we move away from any merely biological understanding of conception. The doctrine is not focused on the biological event and is not tied to any particular theory of conception. There is no implication that Mary was conceived without intercourse between her parents, Joachim and Anne — that is, there is no indication of a teaching of a virginal birth or conception of Mary. The conception of a child is not only a physiological happening, it is also the personal commitment in love of the parents. Such a perception throws an entirely different light on the meaning of conception.

If the term "conception" needs to be reexamined in the ongoing theological dialogue of the various Christian communions, so does the term "immaculate." So often "immaculate" is expressed in terms of being without sin, thus focusing on avoidance of the negative. What proponents of this viewpoint fail to consider is that the Immaculate Conception of Mary, like the sinlessness of Jesus Christ, is not a negative idea but a thoroughly positive and affirmative one. Instead of stating the dogma in the negative form by saying Mary was preserved from the stain of original sin, we may put it in the affirmative way and say she was preserved in a right relationship with God. Another way to express this is to say she was always a recipient of grace.

Given these ways of perceiving the doctrine of the Immaculate Conception, there are some significant points that need to be made. As in all Mariological dogma, we need to see the Immaculate Conception as implicative of Christology and other central doctrines of the Christian faith. Consider these points:

1. We need to deal with objections that this doctrine may encroach on the position of Jesus Christ. One might assume such at first thought, until he remembers a fuller view of child-bearing and motherhood in their total personal sense, not simply as biological relationships. As William P. DuBose wrote, "Christ was born not merely out of the womb, but of the faith and obedience of His Virgin Mother." So the doctrine of the Immaculate Conception, far from detracting from the unique position of Jesus Christ, actually serves to strengthen it.

2. In answer to those who object to this dogma, the official formulation states quite explicitly that Mary's unique grace and privilege in this matter were granted "in view of the merits of Jesus Christ, the Savior of the human race."

3. Mary's righteousness is in faithful obedience to God. Jesus fulfilled the same righteousness, but He is not just the Righteous One, He is also the Redeemer.

4. And in response to criticism that Mariological dogmas infringe on the principle of *sola gratia,* these dogmas do not deflect from the position of Christ. Rather, they consistently point out that Mary's place is due, not to her own merit, but to the gracious election and calling that look toward the Incarnation of her Son.

In summary, we can establish some reasonable arguments that the doctrine of the Immaculate Conception of the Blessed Virgin Mary, far from diluting the centrality of Christ's redemptive work, actually serves to emphasize fundamental doctrines that are acceptable to all Christians.

To appreciate Mariology in proper perspective is to recognize that it is vitally related to our understanding of anthropology, Christology, and soteriology. Scripture, Tradition, and reason are compelling arguments for the entire Christian community to revisit our thinking on this controversy and to recognize the importance, for all Christians, of the doctrine of the Immaculate Conception. In opening, or reopening, our minds as the case may be, we may well be establishing new avenues of communication in the quest for a greater and more meaningful Christian unity.

CHAPTER 10
The Assumption of the Blessed Virgin

By Rev. Peter John Cameron, O.P.

The mysteries surrounding the end of the Blessed Mother's life very much reflect the mysteries that surround the beginning of her life. The feast of the Immaculate Conception celebrates the miraculous entrance of Mary into the world without sin, and the grace-filled power of that event to transform and elevate our conceptions so that we might live in the world in holiness. The feast of the Assumption of the Blessed Mother is very much the same, for this mystery celebrates the miraculous entrance of Mary into heaven, body and soul, and the grace-filled power of that event to transform and elevate our assumptions so that, by the virtue of hope, we might share in that heavenly beatitude even now. So, then, both Mary's coming into the world and her going forth into heaven *affect us now* in our daily living out of faith.

Although this doctrine of faith was defined only as recently as 1950, it is one that has nourished the Church from the earliest centuries. Church feasts commemorating the death of the Blessed Virgin Mary were celebrated in Antioch as early as the fourth century, and in Palestine in the fifth century. St. Gregory of Tours (d. 594) set forth a sound formulation of the doctrine of the Assumption. Pope Sergius I (r. 687-701) introduced several feasts of Mary, including that of the Assumption. There is clear attestation to the idea of the bodily Assumption of Mary in the liturgical and patristic texts of the eighth and ninth centuries, especially in the sermons of St. Andrew of Crete and St. John Damascene. In their scholastic writings, St. Albert the Great, St. Thomas Aquinas, and St. Bonaventure held that the bodily Assumption of Mary was the direct result of her fullness of grace, spoken of in Luke 1:28. Finally, in response to the repeated demands placed on the popes from 1849 onward, Pope Pius XII, on November 1, 1950, formally promulgated that "Mary the immaculate perpetually Virgin Mother of God, after the completion of her earthly life, was assumed body and soul into the glory of Heaven," thereby defining an essential of ancient Catholic Tradition.

It is fair to ask: "What does Mary's Assumption into heaven have to do with my day-to-day living here on earth?" The answer comes partly in the way we regard the term "assumption." In a popular sense, "assumption" means the act of laying claim to something, or taking possession of something. In Mary's glorious Assumption, God lays claim to the body and soul of the Blessed Mother by assuming her miraculously into heaven. But through that Assumption, God wants us to change and conform our "assumptions" about earthly and heavenly life. Mary's Assumption becomes the means by which we can lay claim to divine truths that transform our lives as we possess them in faith. There are three such "assumptions" that the Lord wants us to lay claim to in our lives of faith, which are made evident in Mary's Assumption.

First of all, by Mary's Assumption, God reveals to us that His heavenly graces are meant to permeate every facet of our earthly, creaturely existence — even our very bodies, our flesh and blood, with all their defects, deformities, disfigurements, and imperfections. At times we labor under a false assumption, namely, that God is not interested in our "bodiliness," but rather, only in our souls, the spiritual dimension of our existence.

However, the way God loves Mary, as she is bodily present to Him in heaven, is the way He loves us in our personal relationships with Him here on earth. In Mary's Assumption, God proves that His infinite love is neither selective nor exclusive, but that He loves us in the fullness of the integrity He has given us in creating His children as bodily human creatures. This is the first assumption by which He wants us to live.

In calling Mary to Himself, body and soul, in the Assumption, God reconfirms that His love perfects not only our immaterial souls but also our very material, physical bodies.

In loving us this way, and in demonstrating that love through the Assumption of Mary, God teaches us anew how we are to love ourselves, and the sanctified way in which we are to regard our lives. For, just as God transported and elevated the body and soul of His Mother, so too will He transport and elevate every dimension of our human lives *now* as we remain united with Him in Mary.

This mystery of the Assumption also saves us from *presumption* when we are falsely led to think that we deserve to be loved or treated as special simply because of the way we look. For those moments when the assumptions or presumptions of our lives distract us and wear us down, the fullness of the bodily life Mary enjoys in heaven will console, correct, encourage, and raise us up.

In Mary, the beauty of the whole universe preexists in a mysterious and preeminent way, for she is the Mother of the King of Creation. When we dwell mystically with Mary, holding fast in faith to this mystery of the Assumption, then we realize that God sees in each of us a special perfection and beauty, more precious than the whole material universe created by Him. It is a perfection that comes to fruition as we live in Mary.

Second, it is important to remember that the joy of the Assumption is the result of death — the death of the Blessed Mother, which must have produced a sorrow and grief in the disciples that was surpassed only by the death of Jesus on the Cross.

In our daily lives, we know daily deaths as, over and over again, we are called to die to self and live for God. Many times the false assumption beleaguers us that, if we are suffering, it is because we have done something wrong, or because God no longer cares for us.

In Mary's Assumption, God provides a sure remedy so that this continual dying will not become bitter to us. Mary is the cause of our joy. This is the second assumption God gives us to live by in this mystery. Through the death and Assumption of Mary, the Lord provides the sweetness we need in order to endure our spiritual dying, as well as the sweetness we need in order to see within that experience of death the way to blissful union with God. This assumption also chases away the sinful presumption that true joy can be ours without our sharing in the Cross of Jesus.

And third, the Assumption marks the heavenly inauguration of the communion of saints. In the Assumption of the Blessed Mother, we know our certain hope.

Many times we are duped by the false assumption that our potential holiness is in some way defective. This leads us to believe that we are doomed to an inferior holiness, and not to the resplendent sanctity enjoyed by Mary, the Queen of Saints.

This is where God gives us our third assumption to live by, through Mary's Assumption. God wants us to assume that the holiness and sanctity to which He calls each one of us is a rich sharing in the very glory that the Blessed Mother knows in heaven. However, to hold such a conviction outside the mystery of the Assumption would constitute the sin of presumption.

The glorious adornment of Mary in heaven is the very holiness of all God's saints, as Pope John Paul II asserts when he writes: "In her Assumption into heaven, Mary is as it were clothed by the whole reality of the communion of the saints" (*Redemptoris Mater*, No. 41). Therefore, every justified Christian stands before God as another Mary! All Christian holiness is a direct reflection of the sanctified glory of Mary, Queen of the Saints.

Whatever degree of holiness and sanctity might be possible in this life has already been accomplished in the earthly life and the heavenly life of Mary. Therefore, she is our hope because in her we know not only what we can become but also the maternal love that will bring us to the Father and to the holiness for which we hunger.

God asks that we assume Mary, and the mystery of her

Assumption, into our lives of faith just as He assumes her into heaven. When we are unsure about how to love ourselves in our creaturely condition, Mary is our *life*. When we are troubled by the suffering and sacrifice essential to Christian living, Mary is our *sweetness*. And when we are frightened by anxiety and doubt, Mary is our *hope*.

Hail, holy Queen! Our life, our sweetness, and our hope!

CHAPTER 11
Mary Mediatrix

By Rev. Charles Dickson

Recent articles in *Time* and *Newsweek* magazines report the possibility of a papal dogma on Mary as Mediatrix. However, these secular journals are describing this teaching by using words such as "new," and as an act that would result in a "holy quartet." What the first analysis lacks in knowledge of history, the second lacks in understanding of theology.

The facts are that whether Mary Mediatrix remains a widespread belief among the faithful or becomes a formalized dogma, the concept is neither "new" nor intended to establish a "holy quartet." (It should be noted that no proclamations of dogma are forthcoming at this time. It should also be noted that there is a distinction between the title "Mediatrix," which Catholic theology and popular piety attribute to Mary, and the title "Co-redemptrix," which is accepted in its technical theological meaning, but is not being promoted for wider use because of popular misunderstandings of its meaning.)

There is nothing in all these deliberations that suggests the Church is attempting to place Mary on an equal status with Christ in the act of salvation. Statements to such effect in secular and non-Catholic journals are simply erroneous.

An understanding of Mary as participating in salvation and therefore worthy of veneration was dealt with at the Second Council of Nicaea, which met in 787. This council was responding to an even earlier decree issued by the Church that fostered special liturgical celebrations to honor the Mother of Our Lord.

Among such works were those of the fourth-century bishop St. Ambrose of Milan. Ambrose taught that Mary figured profoundly in the history of salvation and, in a certain way, unites and mirrors within herself the central truths of the faith.

Prior to the time of Ambrose, St. Irenaeus, in the second century, referred to the Church Fathers who saw Mary as used by God not merely in a passive way, but as cooperating in the work of human salvation through free faith and obedience. As Irenaeus stated: "She, being obedient, became the cause of salvation for herself and for the whole human race."

The theme of Nicaea II was reiterated by the Council of Florence (1431-c. 1445) and the Council of Trent (1545-1563), during which cases were made for understanding the Mother of Our Lord as the Mediatrix of human salvation.

This was followed by an encyclical on the Rosary by Pope Leo XIII in 1895, *Adiutricem,* which argued that by her maternal charity, Mary cares for the brethren of her Son who still journey on earth surrounded by dangers and difficulties, until they are led to their happy fatherland. Therefore, the Blessed Virgin is invoked by the Church under the titles of Advocate, Auxiliatrix, Adjutrix, and Mediatrix.

In 1964, at the third session of the Second Vatican Council, Pope Paul VI conferred the title of "Mother of the Church" on Mary in his closing allocution, an address in which he called for veneration of her by stating that the Church is where the Divine Redeemer works salvation, and that the role of the Blessed Virgin is in the mystery of the Incarnate Word and the Mystical Body.

Now the gauntlet has been passed to Pope John Paul II, whose Marian devotion is well-known in both Catholic and non-Catholic communities. Contrary to reports of the secular press, the present pontiff is not dealing with a "new" idea, but one that is carrying more than fifteen hundred years of Christian Tradition.

Nor can belief in Mary as Mediatrix be regarded as an attempt to add another person to the Holy Trinity. The secular press has again missed the mark in accusing the Church of developing what the press calls a "holy quartet." Church teaching throughout history has made it clear that the Holy Trinity remains as the fundamental understanding of the Godhead for

Christians, and the Blessed Virgin Mary, though worthy of our devotion, does not share a position in the Godhead.

Modern clarification on the concept of Mary as Mediatrix is present in an address by Pope Pius XII, when, in a radio message given in 1954, he admonished theologians and preachers of the Word that in treating the unique dignity of the Mother of God, they carefully avoid the falsity of exaggeration on the one hand and the excess of narrow-mindedness on the other. Pope Pius XII was concerned with using the study of Sacred Scripture, the Church Fathers, and other leaders of the Church, so that under the guidance of the Church's teaching authority, we might correctly explain the office and privileges of the Blessed Virgin, which are always related to Christ, the Source of all truth, sanctity, and piety.

This has been followed by the clear pronouncements of Vatican II in which there is ample documentary evidence to indicate that belief in Mary as Mediatrix is to be understood in a way that neither takes away nor adds anything to the dignity and efficacy of Christ, the one Mediator: "The Church does not hesitate to profess this subordinate role of Mary. She — that is, the Church — experiences it continually and commends it to the hearts of the faithful, so that encouraged by this maternal help, they may more closely adhere to the Mediator and Redeemer."

Thus Mary is not seen as being in a position that detracts from the work of Christ, but as the one who makes that redemptive work more powerful and real.

In another portion of Vatican II's proclamation on Mary, the Church recognizes her involvement in the mysteries of Christ. As the most holy Mother of God she was, after her Son, exalted by divine grace, above all men and angels. Hence, the Church appropriately honors her with a special reverence.

In all such pronouncements on the title of Mediatrix, the Council carefully explains the term so as to remove any impression that could detract from the uniqueness and sufficiency of Christ's position as the one Mediator.

As Pope John Paul II contemplates the possibility of a papal proclamation, we cannot predict his decision. However, there are two factors of which we can be sure: He will not be dealing with an idea that can be viewed by any stretch of the imagination as "new," nor will he be contributing to a doctrine that could be interpreted as a "holy quartet."

It is hoped that all of us who belong to Christian communities, especially our leaders, will approach this subject with open minds, recognizing that as we come closer to the Mother of Our Lord, we come closer to her Son.

CHAPTER 12

Our Lady and Cardinal Newman

By Rev. Nicholas Gregoris

(Editor's note: The following is a distillation of Father Gregoris's thesis presented to the Pontifical Faculty Marianum in Rome, for which he earned the degree of licentiate in sacred theology, *summa cum laude.*)

Often one hears people complain that when someone produces a thesis or dissertation, it becomes an exercise in which academics talk to themselves, and no one else ever gets to benefit from the project. With that in mind, I thought it might be worthwhile to share with *The Catholic Answer* readers the results of my study, research, and writing dealing with Cardinal Newman's insights into the place of Mary in the economy of salvation.

Cardinal John Henry Newman, the great convert from Anglicanism of the last century, followed very closely the theological patterns of the Fathers of the Church. In particular, his Mariology can be viewed as a harbinger of the eighth chapter of *Lumen Gentium*. At the outset, however, I should note that I do not intend to become embroiled in the current debate about the proposal that the Pope dogmatically define Mary as Mediatrix, Co-redemptrix, and Advocate. This contemporary angle, nevertheless, has served as a point of departure, and Cardinal Newman might have something to offer this contemporary discussion.

The methodology followed consisted in pursuing three lines of thought: First, to consider Newman's theory of the development of Christian doctrine to demonstrate the connection that exists between Marian doctrine and the living Magisterium of the Church. Second, to treat Newman's theology in relation to Mary's cooperation in the *economia salutis* (the "economy," or plan, of salvation) to show its biblical and patristic roots. Third, to realize that although Newman never wrote a true and proper treatise on Mariology, he did succeed in integrating his Marian theology into his spirituality, giving a particular expression to it through his pastoral ministry.

The Trajectory of Newman's Mariology

How does doctrine develop? We find the answer to that in one of Newman's works, *An Essay on the Development of Christian Doctrine,* in which he expounds on fundamental ideas that are interrelated. The first is that of God's self-revelation, which is confided to the Church like a precious pearl not to be kept in a jewelry box but as the Word of inexhaustible wisdom intended for preaching. The Church is commissioned to engage in this transmission because it has the competence of preaching, authentic and authoritative interpretation, and transmission of the Word of God and the Apostolic Tradition. Newman was convinced that the doctrines of the Church, believed and taught always, cannot change.

That having been said, Newman was very aware that the doctrine of the Church (in all its splendor and richness) cannot be apprehended in one fell swoop. Therefore, he affirms the necessity of a process by which the doctrine of the Church is tasted and digested (so to speak), in "bite-size" portions (for example, the Council of Nicaea, *homoousios*). And so, Newman concludes that it is possible to speak of a theological *evolution*, which never may be equated with a theological *revolution*.

Newman used to compare the way in which ideas of the mind are developed — that is, when these ideas undergo a process of continual reformulation and of gradual perfection without being radically changed — with his idea of the development of doctrine. According to Newman, ideas, like doctrines, are not static. On the contrary, they are full of vitality because they pertain to the eternal reality. It is clear that our formulations of truth are always limited because each is our attempt to capture the unfathomable mystery of God. Truth is not something abstract that remains a simple intellectual proposition; rather, it is a vital relationship that calls for these truths to be accepted intellectually and identified with spiritually.

Newman identified and applied seven characteristics to determine if a particular doctrine was authentically rooted in the faith or was a corruption of it. Although Newman did not apply these principles to Mariology as such, one could use them because aspects of their applicability are especially appropriate regarding the title of Mary as Co-redemptrix.

How does doctrine become dogma? Surveying Newman's corpus, one finds *De Catholici Dogmatis Evolutione* (a work "on the evolution of Catholic dogma"); this should be read in tandem with his *Essay on the Development of Christian Doctrine* to comprehend better the great importance that the concept of the development of doctrine had in his thought. In the former work, Newman was engaged in a dialogue with Father Giovanni Perrone (at the time a professor of dogmatic theology at the Pontifical Gregorian University in Rome); he proposed twelve criteria to determine if a doctrine had the necessary characteristics to undergo a process of "dogmatization."

Another significant contribution made by Newman to dogmatic theology was that of explaining in almost innovative terms the relationship between the Magisterium (*Ecclesia docens*, or "the teaching Church") and the community of the faithful (*Ecclesia discens*, "the learning Church"). *On Consulting the Faithful in Matters of Doctrine* was heavily criticized by some of the most important theologians of his era and was almost rejected by the Holy See. A fundamental concept of this work is that of *conspiratio fidelium et pastorum* (the "breathing together of faithful and pastors"); it does not so much suggest the equality of the two at a magisterial level as that of happy and fruitful collaboration between the community of the faithful and their pastors, both of whom are called to seek and conserve the Deposit of the Faith in their own proper way.

In his famous sermon known as *The Theory of Develop-*

ments in Religious Doctrine, Newman masterfully presents Mary as the exemplar, or "type," of *fides quaerens intellectum* ("faith seeking understanding") who, hearing and contemplating in the most profound way the Word of God (she "kept all these things, pondering them in her heart" [Lk 2:19]), is able to understand its significance and its evolutionary process by making an act of reasoned faith. For Mary, therefore, the knowledge of the truth is not "science" but an authentic hope that flows not so much from her comprehension of truthful propositions as much as from her capacity to integrate these truths into the fabric of her life of faith.

Newman considered the development of the doctrine of the Immaculate Conception a logical consequence of the patristic theology concerning Mary as the New Eve and also a tremendous sign of the ongoing realization of divine providence in the history of the Church. This process of dogmatization of the Immaculate Conception can be viewed as a turning point in the history of the Church, since it was one of the few times when a pope, Pius IX in 1854, explicitly consulted not only the bishops but even the laity of the Catholic world before making a dogmatic definition.

As an apologist, Newman was also concerned with Protestant reaction to Marian doctrine and devotion. His critique of Protestant/Anglican difficulties is found primarily in his famous *Letter to Pusey,* a response to a work written earlier by Edward B. Pusey that was intended to construct a dialogue on disputed points of doctrine between Anglicans and Catholics. In his response, Newman seeks to give answers to the questions posed by Pusey, especially of a Mariological nature.

Newman, in order to defend the Catholic position on Mary, makes numerous references to the Sacred Scriptures and the Fathers of the Church. Newman believed Sacred Tradition to be the most efficacious and convenient argument to enable Catholics and Protestants to find agreement on Marian doctrine and devotion. Newman succeeds in overcoming certain prejudices that Pusey had relative to the Catholic Church; however, Pusey still struggled to accept some devotional expressions that he considered exaggerations of the primitive doctrine about Mary. Newman does not hesitate to point out the abuses that were unfortunately common among some Catholics (for example, in Mediterranean countries) with regard to Marian piety, exaggerations that Pusey deemed to be tainted by an excessive sentimentality and perhaps even superstition.

To take seriously some Protestant critiques, one might imagine that it is a question of Christology versus Mariology. One of Newman's sermons, *The Glories of Mary for the Sake of Her Son,* however, assumes a fundamental theological posture that could be summarized thus: The person and mission of Mary are by their very nature oriented toward the Person and mission of her Son. In fact, Mary depends in everything upon her Son, cooperating with Him to carry out the work of salvation. Their respective roles, however, are never to be confused. Newman attributes to Mary a true and proper cooperation in the *economia salutis,* which the Fathers of the Church describe as free, active, and responsible. At the same time, Mary cannot be opposed to Jesus or said to be in competition with Him as though she were His equal.

Mary's Cooperation as Theotokos and 'New Eve'

Newman, being very attuned to the Scriptures and historically conscious, surveys Mary's place in the *economia salutis* through the prism of the titles of *Theotokos* ("God-bearer," that is, Mother of God) and "Second Eve."

Mary is at the very heart of the economy of salvation. Newman reminds us that the privilege of the divine maternity, or the doctrine of Mary as *Theotokos,* is that privilege from which all other Marian privileges and titles spring and from which they all derive their meaning. St. John Damascene would seem to sum up admirably Newman's thought when he wrote centuries earlier: "The name of the Theotokos contains the whole history of the divine economy in this world."

The patristic doctrine of the New Eve is of fundamental

importance in the theology of Newman and has its roots in the Sacred Scriptures (cf. Gen 3:15; Rom 5:12-20; Rev 12). These biblical roots are not merely figurative or poetic. Rather, they possess a profoundly theological and spiritual character. Newman, following closely the lines of patristic thought, attests to the authenticity and applicability of these scriptural texts, whether at a literary level or the content and meaning of them.

The cooperation of Mary in the work of salvation begins with her Immaculate Conception when, exempt from original sin, she became the antithesis of evil. Besides, Mary is justly called the "New Eve" from the moment of her conception (that is, like the "Old Eve," she was conceived immaculate). However, it is at the Annunciation that this title is put into a greater light as she consents to the divine plan. St. Augustine says: "He Who made you without you, does not justify you without you" (Sermon 169).

Mary ought not to be considered a kind of *deus ex machina* who makes her appearance on the stage of the history of salvation without leaving her own indelible mark. Mary does not *pretend* to cooperate; she *does* cooperate. She is not a sort of biological instrument used by God to bring His Son into the world. Newman tells us that the Fathers of the Church "declare that she was not a mere instrument in the Incarnation such as David or Judah may be considered; she cooperated in our salvation not merely by the descent of the Holy Ghost upon her body, but by specific holy acts, the effects of the Holy Ghost within her soul." Thus, it cannot be said that Mary is in any way extraneous to the *economia salutis;* as Newman declares: "She had a meritorious share in bringing about our redemption."

The *compassio Mariae* (that is, Mary's "suffering with" Jesus), highlighted by Newman in his Marian meditations, can be taken as a notable instance of her cooperation in the work of salvation. By this expression, Newman wants us to understand the precise means by which Mary participated in the passion of Christ. Therefore, Newman affirms in the first place: "She suffered more keen and intimate anguish at our Lord's Passion and Crucifixion . . . by reason of her being His Mother." And again, he writes: "Not in the body, but in the soul, she suffered a fellow-passion; she was crucified with Him; the spear that pierced His breast pierced through her spirit."

All this having been said, we are then led to ask: Did Newman treat of the title "Co-redemptrix"? The answer might seem easy to come by, but it is not for the simple reason that Newman uses the term only once — and in a passing way — when he addresses himself to Pusey as he seeks to remove some of the Anglican's doubts regarding Marian devotion. Newman's response is not easily apprehended because his explanation does not go deep into the meaning of the title, even though it was being used quite fashionably among Catholic theologians in Newman's time while at the very same time it remained highly criticized by Protestant theologians. Hence, it is indeed strange that in his *Letter to Pusey* Newman does not offer a more detailed theological explanation of the title, especially since it was a definite obstacle to Pusey's conversion.

Mary's Spiritual Maternity and Role as Mediatrix and Advocate

Newman upholds the traditional Catholic teaching on the communion of saints. He sees the Church's theology of mediation, its sacramental system, and the cult of the saints as all deriving their efficacy from the more fundamental doctrine of Our Lord's Incarnation. Therefore, Newman affirms that prayer is the greatest expression of an individual believer's participation in the *communio sanctorum* ("communion of saints") and thus renders adoration to God and veneration to the saints. In addition, those who pray can offer their prayers on behalf of the deceased and likewise demonstrate their solicitude and solidarity with the living.

From there, Newman goes on to explain that Mary has always had a privileged place in our collective memory not only because we are mindful of the fact that she cooperated in the work of salvation during her earthly life but also because she cooperates all along by means of her intercession on our behalf. Thus, Newman, citing St. Irenaeus, tells us that we can have recourse to Mary as our "Advocate and friend in time of need."

Newman's meditation on the Cana pericope gives us further insights into the precise nature of Mary's relationship to Christ and His Body the Church. The wedding feast of Cana is a clear example of Mary's cooperation in the economy of salvation, since it is, according to John's Gospel, the first sign performed by Our Lord to inaugurate His public ministry. The mediation of Our Lady at Cana ("Do whatever he tells you" [Jn 2:5]) does not in any way detract from Christ's presence or the efficacy of His actions; on the contrary, her presence places Him and His sign at center stage.

Newman assures us that Mary's prayer is characterized by a unique power, due to her spiritual maternity. By means of her intercession, she is capable of showing us her maternal affection in singular fashion. Newman writes that "while she defends the Church, neither height nor depth, neither men nor evil spirits . . . can avail to harm us, for human life is short, but Mary reigns above, a queen forever."

Thus, for Newman, the title of Mary as *Auxilium Christianorum* ("Help of Christians") merits particular consideration. This title explains in concrete terms the influence of Mary as a result of her numerous interventions in the history of the Church (for example, the Battle of Lepanto and the recitation of the Rosary). The language used by Newman in the litanies of the Name of Mary and of her Seven Sorrows is a clear indication of the attitude of trust and recognition that Christians have always had in her regard. Mary is their Advocate and Mediatrix because she is first the Mother of the Church, that is, their mother.

We might profitably end our reflections by examining what Newman says in his *Memorandum of the Immaculate Conception,* as he carefully distinguishes between what he dubs "The Red Way" and "The White Way." The former refers to the redemptive death of Jesus, which remains an incomparable act of infinite value. The latter calls our attention to the merits of Mary. Or, as Newman synthesizes it: "The obedience of Mary becomes the cause of salvation to all mankind." Mary intercedes on our behalf. Jesus answers her prayers, giving them power and elevating them by His power as our Redeemer and only Mediator. In the final analysis, everything depends on Christ and on His Cross — even the intercessory power of Mary. She is the Mother of the Church because her Son made her so — not because she took this role upon herself as though it were owed her.

Conclusion

Allow me to end this chapter by proposing some possible solutions to the theological problem of Mary's co-redemption. In the first place, one must distinguish between the theology that lies behind the title, the legitimacy of the title itself, and the "opportuneness" of a dogmatic definition of such a title or doctrine.

Concerning the first distinction, I hope to have demonstrated that Newman's thought is not based on a theology of co-redemption, but on a theology of Mary's cooperation in the *economia salutis* — which is precisely the theology of the Second Vatican Council (cf. *Lumen Gentium*, Ch. 8). The title of "Co-redemptrix," although often used by theologians in the past, still lacks theological clarity and thus requires additional study so as to arrive at a deeper and more exact understanding of its meaning.

Regarding the "dogmatization" of a doctrine of Mary as Co-redemptrix, I believe that it is not in reality the opportune moment to make any move in such a direction, given that theological opinions are divided and sometimes too divergent among themselves to be easily reconciled. In my opinion, if Newman were alive today, he would express a judgment against a dogmatic definition, convinced that the theology and title alike are far too ambiguous in the minds of both theologians and the

Magisterium. Furthermore, I suspect that he would offer a *caveat emptor* (as it were) to those who wish at all costs to have the Magisterium exercise its supreme authority by making a dogmatic definition. Newman's attitude toward the extraordinary Magisterium, we should remember, was quite cautious. He believed that it should be a last resort and preferred that doctrines be dogmatically defined only when strictly necessary. It should be noted that Newman thought that the dogmatic definition of papal infallibility was inopportune, although this in no way signified his nonacceptance of this teaching. On the other hand, as already mentioned, Newman expressed much enthusiasm for the dogmatic definition of the Immaculate Conception.

Following the general lines of Newman's thought, I think that if the Church were to define a fifth Marian dogma, it could give greater attention to a doctrine that, much more than co-redemption, has already established its roots in the history of the Church in the development of doctrine. I am referring to the doctrine of Mary's spiritual maternity, explicated by Pope Paul VI in his discourse given at the closing of the third session of Vatican II when he proclaimed Mary *Mater Ecclesiae* ("Mother of the Church"). Perhaps, the Church could more securely follow the example of Paul VI and the Council in defining Mary's spiritual maternity, rather than that of her co-redemption.

In any case, the theological debate about co-redemption remains open and of great moment and can never be concluded if the Church does not first rediscover the full import of the conciliar teaching on the cooperation of Mary in the *economia salutis*. I am convinced that a deepening of the Council's teaching would be of greater importance than any attempt at dogmatization. At the same time, we cannot forget that when Pusey asked for Newman's opinion on the possibility of further Marian dogmatic definitions, the Cardinal responded thus: "The Spirit blows where it wills and cannot be held over for ecumenical peace."

PART 3

Apologetics

CHAPTER 13
In Defense of the 'Theotokos'
By Steven Collison

As one interested in Catholic apologetics, I make it a point to supplement my studies by reading literature and attending conferences sponsored by some of the larger anti-Catholic organizations. Although the Blessed Virgin is a favorite target for many of these groups, I find that they offer little substantive material on the subject of Mary as the Mother of God. Indeed, their lack of effort in trying to debunk Mary as the *Theotokos* (Greek for "God-bearer") is enough to make one think that the Church's opponents are literally speechless on the matter. Yet from time to time, someone will still attempt to dispute the Catholic claim that Mary is in fact the Mother of God; and, sadly, from time to time, the less-instructed Catholic finds the arguments convincing.

One such attempt occurred last year when I attended a conference of Christians Evangelizing Catholics. The speaker who addressed the topic of *Theotokos* as the Church teaches it even went so far as to explain the hypostatic union of Jesus Christ. This surprised me, for it is precisely because of the reality of the hypostatic union that we can call Mary "the Mother of God." Simply put, the hypostatic union is the Person of the Word (the Second Person of the Blessed Trinity) subsisting in two distinct natures: one truly human (received in time from His Mother) and one truly divine (received eternally from the Father). Although the speaker drew an accurate picture of this union, he still drew the wrong conclusions and presented the same old standard charges as to why Mary cannot be the Mother of God.

For someone to believe that Mary is the Mother of Jesus, and that Jesus is both God and Man united in one Person, while at the same time denying that Mary is the Mother of God is remarkable, to say the least. It is like believing that the Father is God, the Son is God, and the Holy Spirit is God, yet denying the doctrine of the Blessed Trinity. The conclusion is inescapable.

Theotokos: A Theological Encyclopedia of the Blessed Virgin Mary states that "the most important truth about Our Lady is that she is the Mother of God." It is because of this exalted vocation that she was privileged with such divine gifts as the Immaculate Conception and the Assumption. Conversely, if God the Son had not become Man, then Mary would have been no different from any other woman. She is not so highly honored by Catholics because of anything in her own right but because of Whom she, and only she, gave to the world — our divine Savior. The importance of being able to explain this truth to non-Catholics cannot be stressed enough. But just as important, it is the first truth concerning Mary that should be presented.

There are two reasons for this. The first is that many Protestants think that the Catholic system of devotion to Mary begins with a faulty exegesis of Genesis 3:15 and snowballs from there into what many non-Catholics see as the monstrous collection of idolatrous Marian beliefs we have today. To show that Marian devotion is legitimately based on her title as Mother of God may help them rethink their position.

Second, Catholic truths are so closely related to and based upon one another that to defend one doctrine without taking the time to explain doctrines upon which that particular teaching is founded would probably be a waste of time. For example, it helps a great deal to explain to non-Catholics the truth of the Real Presence in the Eucharist before tackling the Sacrifice of the Mass. After all, how can one be expected to believe that the Sacrifice of Calvary is being re-presented upon our altars today if he does not believe that Christ is even present on those altars? So it is with Marian beliefs. It is because Mary was to be the Mother of God that she was immaculately conceived so as to be a worthy vessel for the Son of God — the ark of the New Covenant, if you will.

If Catholics do not set forth *Theotokos* as the Church understands the term, our separated brethren cannot be blamed for insistently asking: "Why preserve Mary from sin if she is no different from my own mother?" Of course, we might answer: "Mary is different from your mother because her Child is different from your mother's child." A non-Catholic might retort that she is not the Mother of God but only the Mother of Jesus the Man, or the Mother of Jesus' body or of His human nature, or some similar explanation. This objection is simply untenable and lends no support to the Protestant position. If we are to explain our belief properly, we must labor — happily — to show that Mary is in fact the Mother of Almighty God; and because she is His Mother, we can have the utmost confidence in her prayers for us.

Just as concepts like "substance" and "accidents" are necessary to understand and explain the mystery of the Eucharist, so the concepts of "person" and "nature" are important when explaining the mysteries of the Trinity and motherhood of Mary. They are indispensable tools in ensuring that a Triune God and a Mother of God are believable and not irrational.

By the term "nature" we mean the *permanent* structure of a being, insofar as it is the source of all the activities of that being. In other words, nature answers the question "What is that thing or person?" and decides what that thing or person is capable of doing. Without a nature, nothing can exist. Notice the word "permanent." Jesus is not God by the fact that He is born of Mary, but He is Man for our salvation by the fact that He took His flesh from the flesh of the Virgin. We must always remember that *Jesus is Man* and always will be. He did not just throw on a human nature (as, for example, someone throws on a coat) and then took it off again after His ascension into heaven.

The term "person" defines that self-conscious, rational being that answers the question "Who am I?" It is that reality in a being that says "I." Although the nature is the source of a person's actions, it is the person who is responsible for those actions. For it is the person who possesses the nature and not the other way around. Whatever is done or experienced through a rational nature is done or experienced by the person whose nature it is.

Non-Catholics complain that Mary was not referred to as the Mother of God until four hundred years after Christ. Actually, it was probably closer to two hundred years. Whatever the precise date, we can hardly expect to call Mary "the Mother of God" until we have a clear understanding of exactly Who and what Jesus is. It may well be obvious to us that Jesus Christ was and is one divine Person possessing two natures, and we do not now need any councils or *Theotokos* doctrine to know that. However, as the saying goes, "Hindsight is twenty-twenty." With a two-thousand-year-old tradition of monotheism behind the early Christians, the progression of understanding Christ as both God and Man required the utmost care.

The fact that Mary was seen as the God-bearer is a powerful testimony to the reality of the Incarnation. In the early Church, this fact was used to repudiate several heresies that called the Incarnation into question. Nestorianism claimed that there were two persons in Christ. Monophysitism charged that Jesus had only an appearance of flesh and blood. Monothelitism denied the existence of Christ's human will and claimed that consequently He was not fully human. The Adoptionist heresy taught that Jesus Christ was the Son of God only by adoption and not by nature.

It took the understanding that Mary is the *Theotokos* to arrive at a deeper knowledge of Jesus Christ and, hence, to facilitate the refutation of certain heterodox beliefs. These have always been the primary functions of Mary — to bring Jesus to us and then to bring us to Jesus.

At this point, take a minute to imagine any other ontological combination of person and nature in Our Lord. It is easy to see that if Jesus were, say, two persons, then we could not know for sure that it was God the Son Who died for our sins, and thus not know if we were redeemed or not. If there were no human nature in Christ, then He could not have made an adequate offering for sin on our behalf as a member of the fallen race of Adam. The redemption of mankind depends on the doctrine of *Theotokos*. This frees us from erroneous ideas of what Jesus' mission upon earth accomplished.

It should be enough for "Bible Christians" to believe that Mary is the Mother of God simply by a reading of Luke 1:43, coupled with the knowledge we now have of Jesus Christ as the God-Man. Unfortunately, it seems it is not enough. Yet when Elizabeth calls Mary "the mother of my Lord," she uses a term that, among Hellenistic Jews, meant God. The word is used again in the same way in verses 45 and 46.

Another objection to the unique maternity of Mary is stated thus: Since Mary had no direct role in the joining of these two natures of Christ, she cannot be the Mother of God. Aside from the unforeseen problem posed by that comment — that the Holy Spirit *did* have a direct role in the joining of the human and divine natures, yet He is not the Father of Jesus — such a protestation still does not resolve the question "Whom or what was Mary the mother of?"

A definition of motherhood at this point would be in order. Philosophy tells us that sonship is the origin of a living thing from another living thing by communication of substance unto likeness of nature. Jesus, as Man, fits this definition by receiving His human nature from Mary. Because He fits this definition, we can transpose it (without need for any syntactical gymnastics) to apply to Mary. Motherhood can thus be stated: a living thing that gives origin to another living thing by communication of substance unto likeness of nature.

Can one rightly call her the Mother of God from the mere fact that she gave a human nature to the Person of the Word? Yes, because the relationship of mother to child is not one of nature-to-nature, nature-to-person, nor person-to-nature. It is a person-to-person relationship. Although it is the nature that is communicated, the mother is the mother of the person. No one ever refers to his mother as "the mother of my body" or "the mother of my nature." No, it is always "my mother" or, rarely, "the mother of me." Keeping in mind the hypostatic union and the definition of motherhood, the point to be stressed is that there is exactly one person in the being of Jesus Christ the God-Man. So the person-to-Person relationship between Mary and God (Jesus) is a relation of Mother and Son. Mary is the Mother of God now and forever, since motherhood endures after birth as well as before.

Not only does belief in the divine maternity of Mary protect the integrity of the Incarnation and Redemption, it also reinforces the very truth of the Blessed Trinity itself. The Trinity is revealed to be three distinct Persons in one divine nature. Because Mary is the Mother of the Person of Jesus Christ, she can truly be called the Mother of God, while at the same time not be the Mother of God the Father nor of God the Holy Spirit.

Thus is shown the distinction of Persons within the Godhead. This is just another example of how Catholic doctrine is so intricately interwoven with other revealed truths. To deny even one, needless to say, may lead non-Catholic Christians to deny unwittingly truths to which almost all Protestant communities hold fast.

As it is with any other Catholic teaching, objections to a woman being the Mother of God usually involve an erroneous understanding of what the Church really teaches. A Protestant trying to visualize a Mother of God will probably see in his mind's eye a woman of immense proportions, before eternity (whatever that means), giving birth to divine triplets. This seems to them blasphemous and logically suicidal, as one opponent to the doctrine put it.

The standard argument that reflects this kind of mind-set most clearly is the one that goes something like this: A temporal creature cannot give birth to the eternal Creator.

If this in fact were the Catholic idea of the Mother of God, then it would indeed be blasphemous. It is not the case, however. The difficulty lies in the direction from which the non-Catholic is arguing. It is not Mary who entered eternity; it is God Who entered time. Again, it is not Mary who became the creator; it is God Who became a creature. Mary is no more divine for giving birth to the Eternal Word than the Father is human because He is the Father of the Word Incarnate.

We see that Mary's being the God-bearer has added strength to the truth of the Blessed Trinity. Now the Trinity can return the favor by refuting the objection that Mary is only the Mother of Jesus' humanity, or human *nature*, and not the Mother of God, not the Mother of the *Person* of Jesus Christ. We say that the Father has begotten the Son and is therefore the Father of the Second Person. If we follow Protestant reasoning regarding Mary as the mother of a human nature only, then we would have to believe that the Father is the Father of the Son's nature. This leads us to conclude that the Father is Father of Himself, since there is only one nature among the three Persons. *This* is logical suicide. *Theotokos* is not.

Scott Hahn, a former Presbyterian minister and convert to Catholicism, briefly but brilliantly explains the Church's justification for our devotion to Mary. The first point he sets down is that Jesus Christ fulfilled every letter of the Law perfectly. The first commandment of the Decalogue pertaining to man's obligations to his fellowman is to honor one's father and mother. The word "honor" in Hebrew means "to bestow glory." The second point is that *we imitate Christ*. Hahn concludes that the Catholic Church did not initiate giving glory to Mary; Jesus beat us to it. The beauty of it all is that it is all so simple.

The status of the God-bearer remains irrefutable, if properly understood, and it is up to the instructed Catholic to see that it is properly understood — both by himself and the one to whom he is speaking. After that, maybe other Marian beliefs will not be such hard pills to swallow.

CHAPTER 14
Introducing Mary to Protestants
By Jeffery Dennis

The doctrines of the Blessed Virgin can be powerful and innovative in drawing members of other faiths to Catholicism — but they can also be nearly insurmountable obstacles. Protestants, particularly those in evangelical denominations (Baptists, Methodists, Pentecostals), have been raised to regard any sort of veneration as idolatry; some groups will not even recite the Pledge of Allegiance to the flag. The only images they have ever heard of are the golden calf and Moloch, who demanded the sacrifice of children.

With that sort of background, imagine what happens when a Protestant walks into a Roman Catholic church for the first time and sees a life-size statue of the Blessed Mother. "A graven image!" one friend murmured. "I've always wondered what they looked like."

Not only is the general idea of veneration alien to the average Protestant, but he often finds the special honor given to Mary incomprehensible. Mary is mentioned in Protestant churches only during Christmastime, in reference to the manger of Bethlehem, and perhaps occasionally at Easter, in connection with the many other followers of Jesus; she has no special role to play in the Christian story.

Catholics, caught off-guard by the polite silences or outright accusations of their Protestant friends, often make quick and unthought-out attempts to explain the place of Mary in Catholicism: "Mary intercedes with her Son for us. She's . . . the Mother of God, the Queen of Heaven, and. . . ." Many of the dogmas of the Catholic Church, while profound and vigorous spiritual truths, are couched in technical theological language that sounds quite bizarre to Protestant ears. Here is what your Protestant friend may be hearing when you try to explain the Blessed Virgin the way she was explained to you:

• *The Catholic says:* Mary is ever-virgin. *The Protestant hears:* Mary is a pagan earth goddess. (The non-Catholic remembers the vestal virgins of Rome.)

• *The Catholic says:* Mary was conceived without sin. *The Protestant hears:* Mary is the equal of Jesus. (He remembers that Jesus is sinless.)

• *The Catholic says:* Mary was assumed into heaven. *The Protestant hears:* Mary is the equal of Jesus. (He remembers that Jesus ascended to heaven.)

• *The Catholic says:* Mary is Co-redemptrix. *The Protestant hears:* We don't feel that Jesus is adequate for salvation.

• *The Catholic says:* Mary is our intercessor. *The Protestant hears:* We don't believe that Jesus can do it all.

• *The Catholic says:* Mary is the Mother of God. *The Protestant hears:* Mary gave birth to God the Father. (He uses the word "God" to refer only to God the Father.)

• *The Catholic says:* Mary is the Queen of Heaven. *The Protestant hears:* Mary is God's wife. (Since God is the King of Heaven, Mary must be His wife.)

These interpretations may sound ludicrous and blasphemous, but they are exactly how your Protestant friend will interpret your words. Raised in a world without saints, he cannot conceive of spiritual contact with anyone but a god. You will leave him with the unfortunate misconception that Mary is the chief goddess of a Roman Catholic pantheon, and that Jesus has a minor, almost negligible, role in the Catholic plan of salvation.

The Blessed Mother is rarely met on an intellectual level by people saying, "Oh, yes, I see how the Immaculate Conception is logical"; rather, she is met on an emotional level, as the answer to a subconscious, hitherto unsuspected need. Whenever it is absolutely necessary to explain Catholic doctrines and practices about Mary, try to relate them to secular experiences that we've all had.

Explain the statues by saying, "Do you keep photographs of people especially dear to you? They can be very meaningful by helping you to remember people who are gone. We have no photographs of Mary, of course, so we make statues. We don't worship the statues, just as you wouldn't think of worshiping a photograph. We use the statues to remember Mary, and what she means to all of us."

Explaining that devotion to Mary is in order because she is the Mother of Christ will be meaningless to most Protestants. In fact, the divinity of Christ is often de-emphasized in Protestant churches in favor of His teachings: He came to earth to *tell* us the way of salvation, not so much to *be* the way of salvation. Since Christ as God is not emphasized, the identity of His Mother is unimportant. Instead, explain that devotion to Mary makes sense because she is the first Christian and the ideal that we should emulate in our daily lives. This will be immediately comprehensible and practical to the Protestant, who is often searching for the day-to-day guidance simply not available in even a close and prayerful reading of the Bible. Explain other points of Catholic doctrine in a similar way:

• Instead of saying, "Mary is ever-virgin," say: "Mary dedicated herself to the service of God all of her life, and that, of course, includes her perpetual virginity."

• Instead of saying, "Mary was conceived without sin," say: "In order to fulfill His destiny, Jesus had to be born of a sinless vessel, and that sinless vessel was Mary."

• Instead of saying, "Mary was assumed into heaven," say: "Mary was the first Christian to be taken to heaven, body and soul."

• Instead of saying, "Mary is Co-redemptrix," say: "All Christians have a role to play in the plan of salvation, and Mary as the first Christian has the greatest role."

• Instead of saying, "Mary is our intercessor," say: "To 'intercede' means to pray for someone. We believe that people in heaven can still pray for us, and that applies to Mary first of all."

• Instead of saying, "Mary is the Mother of God," say: "We honor Mary because she is the Mother of Jesus. Since

Jesus is God, we call her 'Mother of God.' This does not mean that she is a goddess; rather, it means that she embodies the great honor that God has chosen to bestow upon humanity."

• Instead of saying, "Mary is the Queen of Heaven," say: "The kingdom of heaven belongs to believers. Since Mary is the first and best Christian, we call her 'Queen of Heaven.' "

The deeper, more profound meanings of these doctrines can come later, through reading or discussions with a priest. For now, it is important to introduce a relationship rather than a list of dogmas. Encourage your Protestant friend to find out as much as he can about Mary in the Bible, about a person whose life reveals to us how to walk in God's presence on a daily basis, and about a person he might have wanted to get to know, if he had been living in New Testament times.

When you take your non-Catholic friend to Mass, encourage him to look at the statue of the Blessed Mother rather than politely ignoring it. And encourage him to imagine her coming down from heaven to fill the church with compassion and love — not to pray to her, in the sense that she is a goddess deserving worship, but to feel a connection with a person present in the first days of Christianity, and who is a conscious being now, a full participant in the Body of Christ.

Novenas, rosaries, the Immaculate Conception, the Feast of the Assumption — all of these can be discussed later. Your goal in introducing a Protestant to the Blessed Virgin should not be to promote doctrine as such, but to introduce a person. Offers to experience the Blessed Virgin, rather than to "understand" her, frequently meet with a new appreciation of Catholicism and a desire to experience more of this Marian aspect of spirituality, which, unfortunately, is blatantly and painfully absent in most Protestant denominations.

CHAPTER 15
Mary: Bridge to Christian Unity

By Rev. Charles Dickson

The agony that a mother experiences when her children are squabbling and fighting among themselves may be a fair analogy to describe the agony the Blessed Virgin Mary must experience amid the quarrels between the disciples of her Son. In view of this, it is not surprising that the bishop of Osnabrück in Germany has suggested that Mary be regarded as the patroness of ecumenism, the rallying point where Christians of all varieties may find unity, common goals, and mutual love.

A significant part of the divisiveness between Catholic and Protestant traditions has indeed been the place of the Virgin Mary in both faith and practice. Yet we must recognize that the split has been magnified beyond its real dimensions by misunderstandings on both sides, with Protestants accusing Catholics of using Mary to replace Christ and Catholics accusing Protestants of completely ignoring her position in Christian history. In the long run, both accusations are unfounded and serve only to splinter further the family of Our Lord at a time when that family needs desperately to pull together.

If healing is to take place, both sides must move beyond the point of polemics and into the arena of honest dialogue. When this happens, we, the sons and daughters of one Lord and Savior, will begin to experience the reality of a family.

While present-day Protestants generally cringe at the suggestion of the Blessed Virgin being a viable part of faith, this was, ironically enough, not a problem for the Protestant reformers. As Lutheran theologian Harding Meyer recently observed, "Luther, Melanchthon, and Zwingli not only did not question teachings about Mary, they explicitly adopted them." These teachings included the Virgin Birth, the doctrine of the *Theotokos* ("God-bearer," that is, Mother of God), the *semper virgo* (perpetual virginity) of Mary, and the sanctification of

Mary as advocated by St. Bernard, St. Thomas Aquinas, and others. And even as practices of Marian piety and devotion emerged, with which they may have had some questions, they did not view them as problems of sufficient magnitude to divide the Church.

Having said this, we now recognize that the arguments about Mary that have served to divide the Christian family are not those that emerged from the concerns of the original Protestant Reformers but rather from the petty bickering that has arisen since their time.

The job for both Catholics and Protestants in our day then becomes one of healing. We need to search diligently for ways of unburdening the Mariological problem that has so splintered our efforts at unity. These efforts are crucial when we realize that our divisiveness not only affects high-level theological discussions but also the everyday lives of the laity in areas as fundamental to life as marriage and the Eucharist. In all these efforts, the Blessed Mother of Our Lord waits with open arms for her children to cease their quarrels and become a family again. She can truly be the bridge for Christian unity.

The starting point for building such unity is the recognition by all that Jesus is our Savior and Lord. Mary, by God's decree, is always a part of that relationship. Jesus was and is God, perfectly human and perfectly divine. Mary, by never being divine or never having been considered a deity, lends her person to being human in the same sense as you and I. She does not belong to Catholics and Orthodox alone. She belongs to all of us who profess her Son as Savior.

The Marian festivals of the early and medieval Church were Christ-centered, and the Reformers wished to continue them. They viewed them as opportunities to focus on the Incarnation and not as some type of evil practice inconsistent with the Christian faith. These included the Purification of Mary, now the Presentation of the Lord (February 2), the Annunciation (March 25), and the Visitation of Mary (May 31), as well as Advent and Christmas. Subsequently, all but the last have been dropped from most Protestant observances and, with this, an opportunity to emphasize not only the central act of the Incarnation but also the role of the Blessed Virgin in salvation history as well.

Luther referred to Mary as "God's workshop" and went on to say, "As the Mother of God, she is raised above the whole of humankind"; she "has no equal." Contrast this with the modern Protestant attitude that criticizes Marian devotion in the belief that it detracts from the central and unique place Christ occupies in human salvation, and one begins to get a picture of the current crisis of division.

What Protestants have had difficulty understanding are the intentions of Catholic teachings about Mary. In the Immaculate Conception and the Assumption teachings, it has not been the intention of the Catholic Church to elevate Mary to divine status but rather to show her as the shining model of Christian hope, indeed the hope for all mankind. Such a re-reading and enlightened understanding on the part of the Protestant community will help to refocus the attention of the entire Christian world on Mary, not as a point of division but as the real bridge of unity for us all.

The Second Vatican Council is slowly but steadily eroding the Protestant misconception that Catholics replace Christ with Mary as the world's redeemer. Pope John Paul II, in a homily at the Basilica of St. Mary Major, said that "Mary's role is to make her Son shine, to lead to Him, and to welcome Him." Such a statement can hardly be conceived of as some form of Mariolatry; rather, it is a genuine expression of a Christ-centered faith made more real by devotion to His Blessed Mother.

What both Catholic and Protestant communities must overcome to accomplish what Harding Meyer calls an "unburdening" of the past is to refocus on the Blessed Virgin as a source of unity rather than division. The basis of this "fundamental consensus" is Mary as the *Theotokos*, or Mother of God, deserving of praise and devotion. Moving from this point, we can allow for the different practices of Marian faith and piety that appear in the Church, and we can exhibit the flexibility that does not view such different practices as worthy of dividing Christ's one, holy, catholic, and apostolic Church.

The Blessed Mother still opens her caring arms as only a mother can do, to welcome all her children back into the one family, which is the Church.

CHAPTER 16
Our View of Mary Should Unite Christians

By Rev. Donald Lacy

Every time I am at the University of Notre Dame, or even in the vicinity, I reflect upon a beautiful and holy lady. Some say she is the biggest source of division among Christians. How can this be? Really, next to her Son, she is the greatest sign of unity.

In reflection and with a bit of mystical vision, I invite you to Holy Scripture and then a hopeful response.

Luke 1:26-38 aids us to launch into a spirit of unity: "In the sixth month the angel Gabriel was sent from God to a city of Galilee named Nazareth, to a virgin betrothed to a man whose name was Joseph, of the house of David; and the virgin's name was Mary" (vv. 26-27).

And all the Baptists confidently affirmed, "We are hearing the Word of God."

"And he came to her and said: 'Hail, full of grace, the Lord is with you!' " (v. 28).

And all the Roman Catholics shouted for joy and proclaimed, "Indeed, that is the way it is"!

"But she was greatly troubled at the saying, and considered in her mind what sort of greeting this might be" (v. 29).

And all the Methodists were socially concerned and sought sincerely to help her.

"And the angel said to her, 'Do not be afraid, Mary, for you have found favor with God. And behold, you will conceive in your womb and bear a son, and you shall call his name Jesus. He will be great, and will be called the Son of the Most High; and the Lord God will give to him the throne of his father David, and he will reign over the house of Jacob for ever; and of his kingdom there will be no end' " (vv. 30-33).

And all the Lutherans boldly confessed, "There is one Christ, true God and true Man."

"And Mary said to the angel, 'How can this be, since I have no husband?' And the angel said to her, 'The Holy Spirit will come upon you, and the power of the Most High will overshadow you; therefore the child to be born will be called holy, the Son of God. And behold, your kinswoman Elizabeth in her old age has also conceived a son; and this is the sixth month with her who was called barren. For with God nothing will be impossible' " (vv. 34-37).

And all the Orthodox chanted in glorious tones, "Truly it is worthy to bless thee, the *Theotokos,* ever blessed and pure, and the Mother of our God."

"And Mary said, 'Behold, I am the handmaid of the Lord; let it be to me according to your word.' And the angel departed from her" (v. 38).

And all the Congregationalists were quick to point out her freedom of acceptance or rejection.

Furthermore, Luke 1:46-55 assists us in our pilgrimage toward unity: "And Mary said, 'My soul magnifies the Lord, and my spirit rejoices in God my Savior, for he has regarded the low estate of his handmaiden. For behold, henceforth all generations will call me blessed' " (vv. 46-48).

And all the Amish thought to themselves, "God has given us a perfect blend of humility, sincerity, and sweetness."

Then Mary continues: " 'For he who is mighty has done great things for me, and holy is his name. And his mercy is on those who fear him from generation to generation' " (vv. 49-50).

And those in the Christian Churches concede, "If we believed in formal creeds, we would really like the message in these words."

" 'He has shown strength with his arm, he has scattered the proud in the imagination of their hearts' " (v. 51).

And the entire evangelical community called out, "Put aside all that heavy theology and simply be born again."

" 'He has put down the mighty from their thrones, and exalted those of low degree' " (v. 52).

And all the Anglicans, agreeing that God's purpose was at work, meditated on Our Lady of Walsingham.

" 'He has filled the hungry with good things, and the rich he has sent empty away' " (v. 53).

And the Presbyterians and Reformed knelt in awe of their sovereign Creator.

" 'He has helped his servant Israel, in remembrance of his mercy, as he spoke to our fathers, to Abraham and to his posterity for ever' " (vv. 54-55).

And all those precious Christians who defy labels and come in a myriad of flavors said, "Amen, amen, amen."

So, you see, Our Lady is a sign of unity and not division. She belongs to all who call her Son Savior and Lord. All who call her Son Savior and Lord belong to her. She is truly "Our Lady for All Seasons."

CHAPTER 17

On Pagan Myth and the Virgin Birth

By Leon McKenzie

It is to be expected that atheists, deists, and agnostics would reject the virgin birth of Jesus. Why is it today that there is little surprise when a Christian leader follows suit? John Shelby Spong, Episcopal bishop of Newark, New Jersey, states emphatically that the virgin-birth tradition is not literally true. "It should not be literally believed," he declares in his book *Rescuing the Bible from Fundamentalism*. Of course, this comment is not surprising coming from the same individual who describes the resurrection of Jesus as something that happened only in the minds of the apostles.

How could the bishop arrive at his judgment about the virgin birth? While he likes to think of himself as a postmodernist, he is a modernist committed to the philosophical dogmas of rationalism and naturalism.

And before we get into the pagan myths centered around the virgin birth, let us look at recent philosophical developments that lead to claims that the virgin birth could not have actually occurred.

Modernists generally presume that a transcendent God does not, and cannot, enter the world of ordinary experience — miracles cannot happen; wonders do not exist; unexplainable events are really misunderstood events. If they believe in God at all, they suppose that long ago God created the cosmos but has not interfered with its laws since.

Rationalism, a subset of modernism, is based on the assumption that human reason is autonomous, a law unto itself, and eminently supreme. Divine Revelation is ruled out, or interpreted as manifesting itself solely through human reason. Usually, the model of rationality adopted by modernists constricts the notion of possibility to what each particular rationalist is capable of imagining.

Naturalism is the doctrine that excludes the reality of the supernatural order or the agency of any supernatural being in the workings of the world — another subset of modernism. What exists is the raw universe, available to the senses; natural laws control everything. They are defined as rigid rules that cannot be evaded. Everything in human experience is attributed to the strict regimen of natural causality.

Although Bishop Spong characterizes his thinking as postmodern, his theological positions are suggestive of a stagnant nineteenth-century ideology that has been critiqued effectively by the better representatives of postmodern thinking.

The word postmodernism is often used to connote so many things that it is almost futile to assign it a definite meaning. Those who understand the roots of postmodernism, however, know that one of its positive aspects is its critique of modernism.

Far from exemplifying the cutting edge of current thought, most rationalists and philosophical naturalists today give voice to an outdated philosophy. This failed worldview cannot meet the challenge of the postmodern norm of openness to the wide range of reality's possibilities and a reexamination of what is worthwhile in the past.

A more current model of rationality recognizes the importance of imagination in the thinking process. Many individuals, I propose, reject "marvelous" happenings because they are ill-equipped to visualize these events. Their powers of imagination have been sapped by a Western culture that for three hundred years or more has grasped reality as an inert physical object and not as a source of mystery that invites wonder.

Modernists offer differing reasons for rejecting the actual virgin birth of Christ. Two of the principal arguments are considered here.

First, virgin births simply do not happen; they are contrary to scientific laws and human reason. Second, myths of virgin births were around for centuries before Christ. The virgin birth of Jesus is "nothing but" another myth. Thus does facile reductionism displace research and analytical thinking.

Who Defines the Limits of Possibility?

Rationalists and naturalists constructed a model of the world that made its movements consistent and predictable. This work was furthered most prominently by Isaac Newton (1642-1727). "To the ancients the world was a living organism," wrote the eminent scientist John Barrow, "but to Newton and his followers it was a unified mechanism — like a giant watch. Its workings were pristine: precise, mechanical, and mathematical."

The notion of the world as a machine reached a flowering in the nineteenth century. The world, after it was created by God, moved according to its own rules. Not even God, it was maintained, could intervene to act against the laws of nature.

Presuming that laws of nature were fixed and unalterable, births occurred in a specified manner that admitted no exception. The virgin birth of Jesus was impossible in terms of modernist doctrine. Human reason, answerable to no greater Mind, drew up the definition of the limits of possibility.

Recently, however, some theoretical scientists and philosophers have proposed that laws of nature are not regulations inherent in the world, but are simply our changing descriptions of the way the world appears to function.

The question has been seriously asked if natural laws of the physical world could exist everywhere except for certain times and places. For example, Albert Einstein's law of gravitation, according to Barrow, has "the property of predicting there can arise states in which its jurisdiction does not apply. It predicts that it cannot predict."

According to mathematical theorems in physics, singularities exist under certain conditions. The universe contains places where the laws of nature seem inoperative. This, by the way, is not science fiction — here, however, is not the place to wander knee-deep in theoretical physics.

Could it have happened that the ordinary laws of sexual reproduction did not apply in the case of Jesus' birth? Were His birth, miracles, and resurrection singularities in the sense of physics? Speculations such as this are intriguing, but unnecessary for faithful Christians.

Christians have always believed — without the endorsement of scientists — that God is the Lord of the cosmos and of history, the God for Whom all things are possible (see Mk 10:27). God is the Author of the laws of nature — however defined — that guide what regularly happens in the ordinary world. He has the authority to make any changes He desires in governing the universe He created. God alone defines the limits of what is possible.

Pagan Birth Myths

Pagan myths of exceptional births can be seen as expressions of an obscure hope for a savior. This hope was placed within the human breast by the Creator. These myths flourished in the ancient world. Exceptional heroes — especially those who supposedly rose from the dead and/or worked wonders — would be expected to enter the world in an exceptional manner. Stories of miraculous births were usually bizarre, sometimes silly, and often indecent, but they dramatized in a muddled way the pagan hope for someone who would come to deliver them from the darkness of meaninglessness.

What are these myths? What are their characteristics? A review of three of these stories may be helpful in providing a taste of their essential character. The myths presented here are abstracted from *The Golden Bough,* the classic work of Sir James Frazer, and Jack Finegan's scholarly work *Myth and Mystery.*

Dionysus • The Greek god Dionysus, known as Bacchus to the Romans, perhaps found his origin as a mythic figure in the primitive tribes of Thrace, who valued drunkenness as a form of worship. Dionysus was the opposite of the god Apollo. Apollo represented order, rationality, and moderation; Dionysus was worshiped as the patron of frenzy, wild exuberance, and excess.

Zeus took the form of a snake and had intercourse with the goddess Persephone. She gave birth to Dionysus, who was a horned infant. He took many forms when necessary to protect himself from the malice of the other gods. Once he took the form of a bull, was slain, and cut to pieces by his enemies. His severed limbs were buried by Apollo. It is recounted that his body was pieced together and he was restored to life. The tearing apart and eating of live bulls seemed to be a main feature of wild Dionysian rituals. As with most myths, there are contradictory versions of the god's "resurrection." His miraculous birth was distinctive in that Zeus became a serpent to have intercourse with Dionysus' mother.

Attis • Attis was the Phrygian counterpart of the Greek Adonis. It is told that his mother, Nana, conceived him by putting a ripe almond in her bosom. In Phrygian cosmogony the almond was considered the father of the world. Sir James Frazer observed that the almond's blossom was one of the first heralds of spring. As such, the almond was probably a magic charm worn by women who wished to become fertile.

The "resurrection" of Attis was unusual. One myth recounts that Attis mutilated his genitals under a pine tree and bled to death. The story attempts to explain why the priests of Attis mutilated themselves during the great celebration of his feast each year. Attis rose from the dead each year in the form of a pine tree. On his feast in March, as nature itself was arising from the death of winter, the devotees of Attis cut down a pine tree, brought it to his temple, and treated it as a divinity.

Osiris • The birth of the Egyptian god Osiris came about through the intercourse of the earth-god Geb and the sky-goddess Nut. Nut was also the wife of the sun-god Ra. The earth-god Geb, according to Finegan, is visualized prostrate as the flat earth while the sky-goddess Nut is pictured as bowed over the earth, Geb, with her feet resting on the eastern horizon and her hands on the western horizon supporting her weight.

Osiris, the hero king of Egypt, was not the only the child of Nut. The sky-goddess, it was claimed in one version of her myth, was the mother of the sun-god. She swallows him in the evening in the west and bears him each morning in the east. This myth shows a strong connection between the concepts of miraculous births and resurrections or rebirths of various gods. Osiris was said to have been cut into pieces and miraculously put together again to reign as the lord of the netherworld.

Pagan Myths: An Assessment

The myths described above refer to gods who never actually existed. The first big difference between these stories and the account of Jesus' virgin birth is that myths happened "once upon a time," not historically. Myths do not pretend to be anchored definitively in a specific time or place.

The second difference between myths and the account of the virgin birth of Jesus is found in the exorbitantly fantastic details of the births of gods and heroes. The accounts of these births are more ludicrous than credible, more banal than serious. The myths possess not a whiff of anything even approaching truth. They are marked with an overwhelming character of absurdity.

The virgin birth of Jesus is reported briefly, discreetly, and absent of the kind of surreal details associated with myths.

There are usually many versions of the same myth. Each different ancient culture worshiped some of the same gods under different names. Accounts of their deeds vary considerably even within one distinct culture. In addition, there are often modern forgeries of ancient myths by those who hope to win debater's points in religious arguments.

The story of Mithras, for example, who was "born" on December 25 (the winter solstice in the old Roman calendar), is frequently manipulated to resemble New Testament accounts of the Christian Nativity. Interpolations are made by contemporary anti-Christian polemicists that include visits by three kings and even by shepherds to the infant Mithras, whose "birth" is never mentioned, save in terms of his imaginary return with the sun at the winter solstice.

In an article in one openly anti-Christian periodical, I counted eighteen instances of direct compatibility — in one paragraph! — between the story of Christ's birth and the "birth" of Mithras. I could find these details in no other source. The forgery was obvious. This doctoring of the tale of Mithras promoted the argument that Jesus is "nothing but" the mythic hero known as Mithras.

One may reliably conclude that mythic accounts of miraculous births bear no resemblance to the Gospel accounts of the virgin birth of Christ. Myths of miraculous births of exceptional individuals, however, are not illogical among ancient peoples given to mythological thinking. These myths, in God's providence, prepared the way for belief in the virgin birth of Jesus on the part of pagan converts to Christianity. Remember, the human psyche from which these myths emerged was created by the all-provident God, Who gave signs of hope from the earliest times, according to St. Augustine, to even our ancient ancestors we know today as pagans.

But why should there have been a virgin birth of Jesus at all?

The Virgin Birth of Jesus
The resurrection of Jesus is the normative event for the interpretation of pagan resurrection myths. Pagan myths of renewal do not explain Jesus' resurrection. The resurrection of Jesus is the decisive event in history that explains why resurrection myths should have occurred at all.

So also is the virgin birth of Jesus normative for understanding pagan myths of marvelous births. If a god was said to have risen from the dead, or if a mortal was declared divine and immortalized by law or popular acclaim, it is likely the god or human was also said to have had a miraculous birth. *The experience of rebirth from the dead implied an original birth that was of all-surpassing importance.* If someone is manifested as some sort of a savior, it was concluded that person must have been a savior from the moment of his birth.

The brief New Testament accounts of the virgin birth of Jesus are delicate and almost respectfully hushed out of regard for the mystery itself and, most likely, out of sensitivity for Mary's modesty. The belief of the early Christian community in the virgin birth of Jesus was stated very early. Not only is it reported in Matthew and Luke, but it was also an article in the Roman creed used in early baptismal ceremonies.

The final edited versions, or redactions, of Matthew's and Luke's Gospels are usually dated around A.D. 80-90. This does not mean that all of the material in the Gospels dates from that time. Materials from much earlier times — liturgical formulas, the "sayings" of Jesus, and oral traditions — were incorporated into the Gospels when they were finally redacted.

Hippolytus wrote a treatise on the Apostolic Tradition around 213. Some of the source material contained therein reflects creedal articles that were used in Rome close to the beginnings of the Church's existence. One of the articles in this early form of the Apostles' Creed refers to the virgin birth of Jesus.

No one can say with certainty how the narrative about the virgin birth of Jesus and creedal statement came to be formulated, and thereafter included respectively in the New Testament and the Apostles' Creed. It is not improper, however, to imagine a hypothetical scenario.

The Tradition of the Virgin Birth

When Mary was greeted by the angel Gabriel at the Annunciation, she was completely in tune with the will of God, completely committed to the Word of God transmitted by Gabriel, and completely obedient to God. She was the model believer for the early Christian community. She accepted God's plan without question. She responded to Gabriel's message — that she was to become the Mother of the Messiah by exceptional means — in a direct and simple manner. "Behold, I am the handmaid of the Lord; let it be to me according to your word" (Lk 1:38).

The virgin birth of Jesus is connected inextricably to the resurrection of Jesus. Jesus was made manifest as Lord in His post-resurrection appearances to the apostles and other disciples. It was only after His resurrection, and after the descent of the Holy Spirit on the apostles and disciples, I believe, that Mary gained full insight into the meaning of the extraordinary circumstances of her Son's conception and birth. She always knew He was a very special person. She probably did not know He was the Son of God — really, not simply in figurative language — until after the Resurrection.

Mary placed her faith in God when Jesus was conceived in her womb, and when He was born. She trusted God when she listened to the prophecy of Simeon, and when she and Joseph found Jesus in the Temple in a discussion with the teachers (see Lk 2:41-50). She committed herself to God during Jesus' public life when He worked wonders and said things the authorities did not want to hear. Mary relied on God at the time of Jesus' sufferings and death, despite possible painful feelings of confusion.

The seven sorrows of Mary, upon which we meditate when praying the Seven Dolors Rosary, were not pretenses. Her sorrows were profound, but she went forward trustfully, not knowing fully what the outcome would be. Her trust in God was rewarded with deep insight at the time of the Resurrection, when her Son was made manifest as Lord, and more clearly so at Pentecost under the guidance of the Holy Spirit.

After the birth of Jesus, Mary kept turning over in her mind the astounding events surrounding His birth. There is no other passage in the New Testament that appears to be an explicit source citation, in my judgment, than the words of Mary when she marveled at the praise of the shepherds at the Nativity. "But Mary kept all these things, pondering them in her heart" (Lk 2:19).

The resurrection of Jesus revealed Jesus as Lord, but some

may have thought Jesus was merely adopted as God's Son at that time. (The heresy of Adoptionism, in fact, did rear its head later.) A tactful question to the Mother of Jesus by one of the women disciples was all that was needed. A modest nod and a few words from Mary would have been enough to establish the actuality of the virgin birth. This entered into the oral tradition and was eventually stated by Luke in his Gospel.

The Relevance of the Virgin Birth

The virgin birth of Jesus is a sign that conveys the reality of the Incarnation. As a sign, it shows the discontinuity between Jesus and fallen humanity. In the words of Carol Zaleski, in *The Life of the World to Come,* in Jesus was effected "God's own sacrificial descent into our mortal condition."

While Jesus was made manifest as Lord in the Resurrection, He was not simply a human person God adopted to play the role of Lord. Jesus is the eternal Word of God in Whom and with Whom all things were created. He was not chosen by God to enact a role in the drama of salvation, but was the pre-existent Word, Who became flesh in His mother's womb.

The virgin birth of Jesus was not simply a wondrous event. It was not something accomplished to amaze people as a magician dazzles his audience. The virgin birth was an act of revelation by which God disclosed something about His divine and eternal Word.

The late Scripture scholar Bruce Vawter, C.M., wrote that it is more congenial for some scholars nowadays to view the infancy narratives as simply "wonder stories." Profession of belief in the virgin birth, I suggest, is not "religiously correct" in today's secular culture, which is rife with the presumptions of modernism. He also maintained we are not in any position to evaluate historically the details of these narratives. Elements of wonder and the theological purposes of the inspired authors of the Bible "do not automatically exclude the factual plausibility of an alleged event." Vawter's comments are discerning and penetrating.

No one can "prove" the virgin birth of Jesus. It can be argued effectively, however, that the virgin birth is not impossible. It can be shown as worthy of belief. After this, the individual is offered the option of saying yes or no to the teaching of the Catholic Church, the testimony of Sacred Scripture, and the affirmation in the Apostles' Creed. Before that "yes" or "no" is uttered, it should be recalled that faith is an intellectual problem only to a certain point in the journey toward God. After that point has been reached, faith is no longer an intellectual quest but instead a matter of spiritual concern.

CHAPTER 18

A Protestant Discovers Mary in the Bible

By Robert Sungenis

In my travels as a Catholic apologist, I happened upon a conversation with a Protestant who was considering joining the Catholic Church, but who found the doctrines of Mary to be a huge stumbling block. She gave me the usual objections: Catholics worship Mary; the Bible doesn't tell us to pray to Mary; Mary had other children besides Jesus; Mary was a sinner like everyone else; and so on. She was particularly disturbed at the numerous Marian apparitions that have surfaced in the last few years and wondered if these were not just manifestations of the devil.

As any Catholic does when a Protestant confronts him with questions about Mary, he takes a deep breath, listens sympathetically, and then tries to explain as best he can one of the hardest teachings of the Catholic Church for non-Catholics to understand and accept. Indeed, doctrines of Mary are usually the last obstacle overcome by Protestants who join the Catholic Church. Why? There are two main reasons: (1) There just isn't that much information in the Bible about Mary. For those who are used to obtaining their convictions from Scripture alone, the Catholic claims for Mary seem unsubstantiated, if not heretical. (2) To Protestants, some of the recent Catholic pronouncements about Mary appear to make her a savior right alongside of Jesus — for instance, one pope declared that "all graces come through Mary." In addition, various Latin American and Eastern cultures seem to treat Mary like a god rather than a human being. Protestants don't have an aversion to Mary, per se, but they feel an obligation to stop what they see as blasphemy against God.

Now, in this short chapter I am not going to answer all the objections Protestants have against Mary. There are plenty of books and articles that address those objections. Father Peter Stravinskas has written an excellent work in this regard called *Mary and the Fundamentalist Challenge,* which is published by Our Sunday Visitor. I will, however, give you some "psychological" hints on how to approach Protestants and their objections to Marian doctrine, as well as show you how to use what little information Scripture contains about Mary to advantage. The best way to do this is allow you to "listen in" on the conversation I had with my Protestant friend. Though I've added a few things to fill in the gaps, much of this conversation actually took place.

KATHLEEN: Robert, I'm really considering becoming a Catholic, but Mary is by far the most difficult area for me as an evangelical, *sola Scriptura* (Scripture alone) person. I have a Catholic bookstore near me, and I picked up a couple of books on Marian devotion so that I can try to understand.

ROBERT: I admire your effort to grapple with these issues. I know it's hard. I used to be a Protestant myself. Mary gave me the hardest time before I converted to Catholicism.

KATHLEEN: Thanks. I started to read a book called *The History and Devotion of the Rosary.* It contains a chapter on Fátima, which I understand the Church has approved. Here are some quotes from Mary given at Fátima that really give me a problem!

ROBERT: OK, let's hear them.

KATHLEEN: All right. Here's the first one: "Jesus wants to establish devotion to my Immaculate Heart in the world. I will never leave you: my Immaculate Heart will be your refuge and the way that will lead you to God."

ROBERT: What's the problem with this?

KATHLEEN: Well, I think of the words of Jesus, Who tells us that He is our refuge, our fortress, that we are to worship only God — that He is a jealous God. Mary comes along and claims that only she can save the world from war? That a chapel must be built in her honor? That if someone jumps through all the right hoops of saying the Rosary on certain days, etc., that then she will give that person grace for salvation?

ROBERT: But Kathleen, listen to what Mary is really saying. Mary speaks of "devotion," not worship, so you can't claim there is any competition with God. Mary's heart is "immaculate" because, according to Church teaching, she was sinless. Even your Protestant forefathers, Martin Luther and John Calvin, believed that much about Mary. There is nothing wrong with taking "refuge" in Mary, since we also take refuge in the Church, in prayer, in repentance, etc. When we take such refuge, we understand that it is not due to the power inherent in the intermediary, but in the power God gives to the intermediary. Mary is not upstaging Jesus. She specifically says that Jesus wants her to establish devotion.

KATHLEEN: She also says, "Continue to say the Rosary every day in honor of Our Lady of the Rosary to obtain peace for the world and the end of the war, for she alone can save it."

ROBERT: Again, Mary doesn't speak of worship, but of "honor." When she says "for she alone can save it," she doesn't mean that by her own power, apart from God, she can end war. From her other approved apparitions we know she means God is ready to judge the world for its sins and one of those judgments could be war. She tells us that it is mainly her pleading with God that moves Him to hold back His wrath, not unlike Abraham's pleading for Sodom and Gomorrah.

KATHLEEN: Well, how about when she says, "I want to tell you that they must build a chapel here in my honor."

ROBERT: Same difference, Kathleen. We are not giving her worship, only honor. As we honor our father and mother according to the Fourth Commandment, we honor Mary. Don't you think she ought to receive some honor for bringing Christ into the world? And what occurs in a chapel? Nothing but prayer, sacrifice, and worship to God through the Mass and the sacraments.

KATHLEEN: I don't have a problem with that. But then she says, "I promise to assist at the hour of death with the grace necessary for salvation for those who, on the first Saturday of five consecutive months, go to confession and receive Holy Communion, recite the Rosary, and keep me company for a quarter of an hour while meditating on the mysteries of the Rosary with the intention of making reparation to me."

ROBERT: No problem here, Kathleen. Mary is giving her "assistance," not a divine fiat. She "assists" by being an intercessor. According to Church teaching, the grace Our Lady gives is that which comes from God, not from Mary herself. A priest can also "assist" and "give grace" at the hour of death under the power of the sacrament of the anointing of the sick or sacrament of penance. Since he is specially ordained of God for such purposes, he can assist in ways that other people cannot. Similarly, because Mary is specially endowed by God as an intercessor, she can assist in ways not common to other people or even priests. As for "making reparation," Mary does not mean that we are to make a restitution to her, anymore than the priest who gives absolution and requires penance in the confessional is directing the reparation toward himself.

KATHLEEN: For many years, I've gone directly to Jesus, and He has so greatly blessed me with His sweet presence and many miracles — like being instantly healed of breast cancer in 1991. There is no suggestion in Scripture that we must go through Mary to get to Him — it's just not true, and I feel that, in the Church, Marian devotion or veneration has moved into the area of blasphemy.

ROBERT: Kathleen, by the logic of your own argument I can show where you are wrong.

KATHLEEN: OK, I'm open to see it. I hope you can, because I really do want to become Catholic.

ROBERT: You prayed to Jesus, and He cured you of breast cancer in 1991. But why did you have to pray to Jesus?

KATHLEEN: What do you mean?

ROBERT: Didn't Jesus know that you had breast cancer and needed to be healed? He's God, and He knows everything, but He still required you to pray, didn't He?

KATHLEEN: Yes, I can't argue with that.

ROBERT: That tells us something very important about God. Often He won't do something because no one prays to Him. St. James teaches us the same thing in those Scriptures you rely on so heavily. In James 4:2 it says, "You do not have, because you do not ask [God]." In 1:5-7 he says, "If any of you lacks wisdom, let him ask God . . . and it will be given to him. But let him ask in faith, with no doubting. . . . For that person must not suppose that a double-minded man . . . will receive anything from the Lord."

KATHLEEN: So what you're saying is that without prayer God won't give us what we desire?

ROBERT: Well, of course, God can do whatever He wants, but He does make a point to tell us that we will not receive from Him unless we pray. God has set up prayer as the vehicle to do His bidding, and He will not change it.

KATHLEEN: OK, but how does this answer my questions about Mary?

ROBERT: I'm not finished yet. Let me take you to some other Scriptures in that Protestant Bible of yours. In 1 Timothy 2:1-4, St. Paul says, "First of all, then, I urge that supplications, prayers, intercessions, and thanksgiving be made for all men, for kings and all who are in high positions. . . . This is good, and it is acceptable in the sight of God our Savior, who desires all men to be saved and to come to the knowledge of the truth." Here, St. Paul says that we must make prayers and intercessions to God for everyone. Why? Because God wants all men to be saved; and prayer is the means through which God will grant them salvation. We can conclude that if we don't pray for them, it will affect whether or not God saves them. Do you see how important intercessory prayer is, Kathleen?

KATHLEEN: Yes, I knew it was important, but I never considered that a lack of prayer could result in someone's not being saved. But it does make sense. Why would God command us to pray if our prayer really didn't affect the outcome?

ROBERT: Right! That's why so much emphasis is put on prayer and intercession in Scripture. Essentially, if we neglect to pray for another person, God may not act on his behalf. First, we saw that God requires you to pray to Him directly; now we see that God requires intercessory prayer. According to Catholic teaching, even souls in purgatory can languish because no one prays for them.

Think about it this way, Kathleen. God could have easily created the world without a need for prayer or intercession. He certainly knows everyone's need before it occurs, but God delights in "Christian solidarity." He could just snap His fingers and have everything done. However, in His infinite wisdom, He chose not to design things that way, and He will not change it. If God did change it, then He would be dishonoring Himself. In effect, in order to maintain His own honor and veracity, God requires prayer and intercession in order to act on our behalf.

KATHLEEN: Wow! I knew we had responsibility, but I just didn't realize it was that serious!

ROBERT: That's right. Now you're catching on. But an equally important part of prayer and intercession is that we use the vehicles God has ordained to bring prayer and intercession to Him.

KATHLEEN: What do you mean?

ROBERT: First, in James 5:16-18, Scripture tells us that God will listen to the prayers of a righteous man. He uses the example of the righteous prophet Elijah, who prayed to God that it would not rain. In answer, God withheld the rain for three-and-a-half years.

KATHLEEN: You mean God will answer the prayers of some people more than the prayers of others?

ROBERT: Yes. God listens to people who live righteous lives, and He is moved to answer their prayers. Proverbs 15:8 says, "The prayer of the upright is his delight," and in 15:29, "He hears the prayer of the righteous." The more righteously we live, the more God is pleased with us and the more He will answer our prayers. Conversely, if we sin, then God may not hear our prayers, admonishing us: "When you spread forth your hands, I will hide my eyes from you; even though you make many prayers, I will not listen" (Isaiah 1:15). In 1 Peter 3:7, husbands are warned that if they mistreat their wives, God will not listen to their prayers.

KATHLEEN: I guess I have to adjust my Protestant thinking a little.

ROBERT: Yes, it's quite a paradigm shift. You have to stop thinking that everyone's righteousness is the same, a belief that stems from your Protestant doctrine of "imputed" righteousness. You need to start thinking that there are people who are more righteous than you because they actually live that way — under the power of God's grace, of course.

KATHLEEN: So where does this lead us?

ROBERT: Well, if I know my saintly intercessors are more righteous than I by the mere fact that they have already made it to heaven, and if I know that God listens to the prayers of righteous people, then it is only logical that God will answer the prayers of my heavenly intercessors, perhaps more often than He will answer mine.

KATHLEEN: I do follow your logic. This is certainly interesting. But can we get back to Mary? I really want to know how she fits into all this.

ROBERT: No problem. Mary is one of those people who is more righteous than you or I. In fact, Mary is sinless. It is no wonder that God encourages us to seek her intercession when we desire something from Him. God is greatly affected by the prayers of holy people. The best example I can think of from Scripture is in Exodus 32:9-14. God wanted to destroy all of Israel after they worshiped the golden calf. Moses, whom God considered a righteous man, prayed that God would relent in his anger. Verse 14 records one of the most amazing responses in Scripture: "And the Lord repented of the evil which he thought to do to his people." Later, in Exodus 33:11-19, God says that He listened to Moses' prayer because Moses was God's friend; Moses pleased God, and God knew Moses by name. In modern terms, God answered Moses' prayer because God liked Moses very much.

KATHLEEN: That's amazing. I really see the effect prayer can have on God. But can you give me more help? It's really a big step for me to pray to someone like Mary.

ROBERT: Let me put it this way. The proud person claims that he doesn't need any of the intermediaries or vehicles God has established. He thinks that he is righteous enough to go directly to God without any support from others, without any sacraments, without the Church and its communion of saints. He thinks he is honoring God by bypassing intercessors, but in reality, he is dishonoring God and puffing himself up. It's one thing to pray to God by yourself, but when you insist that you don't need intercessors to pray for you, then you really don't understand prayer at all, or what truly pleases God.

KATHLEEN: I never looked at it that way before. I guess my Protestant "rugged individualism" made me think that it had to be "just me and Jesus." I can see that due to our Protestant belief in the "imputed covering of Jesus" we think everyone is on the same level with God, but I'm beginning to see that that is very wrong. I have to admit that the Israelites in Exodus 32 were certainly not on the same level with God as Moses was. I just didn't believe there could be anyone more righteous than myself on whom to depend for answers to prayer. Wow! How self-centered I've been!

ROBERT: Bingo! Now, if the Church, acting infallibly on God's behalf, declares Mary to be one of the chief intercessors before God, then it would behoove us to use her as a conduit, or God may not answer our prayers. Now don't misunderstand me. It's not that God doesn't have the power to do things without Mary. Remember, God could snap His fingers and do anything. It's because God has already set up Mary as our heavenly intercessor, and He cannot go back on His word. In effect, rather than blaspheming God when you pray to Mary, you are giving God the deepest honor possible, because you are recognizing and utilizing the vehicles of grace that He has established.

KATHLEEN: I never thought that my solitary appeals to God could be a sign of pride. That's amazing!

ROBERT: Yes, as St. Paul says in 1 Corinthians 3:18, "If any one among you thinks that he is wise in this age, let him become a fool that he may become wise." Intercessors, such as Mary, may seem silly to Protestant sensibilities, but I guarantee that she is the key to prayer and power with God. Although He is powerful enough to do anything He desires, nevertheless, in His infinite wisdom, He has chosen to accomplish His works through select channels and intermediaries, and He will not change it. Anyone who wants to continue to have God's ear must recognize this principle.

KATHLEEN: Wow, Robert. Thanks a lot. You've really opened up my mind. I guess I'll have to go home and start praying about all this.

ROBERT: When you do, offer prayers to Mary. She'll call on God's grace for you so that you'll understand a lot faster and a lot better.

PART 4

Marian Prayer and Devotion

CHAPTER 19

Mary Leads Us to Christ

By Rev. Jay Scott Newman

(Editor's note: The following is a homily preached by Father Jay Scott Newman, on March 25, 1998, the Solemnity of the Annunciation, at Lenior-Rhyne College in Hickory, North Carolina, a college of the Evangelical Lutheran Church in America.)

My name is Jay Scott Newman, and I am a disciple of Our Lord, Jesus Christ. I am also, by the grace of God, a priest of the New Covenant in the presbyterial order. But this was not ever so. Indeed, I was not always a Catholic, and how I came to be is part of my tale.

I was born in North Carolina to a family of Baptists and Brethren, but when I was thirteen, I announced to my startled parents that I was an atheist. In part to escape the Christ-haunted South, which was then a great nuisance to me, I fled North to study, and it was during my undergraduate studies that I — to my everlasting wonderment — was converted to faith in God in Christ.

I was baptized in the Episcopal Church, and my sponsors were a Lutheran woman and a Methodist man. But, almost immediately, I was drawn to the Catholic Church by the power of the liturgy, the majesty and clarity of the teaching, and the person of Pope John Paul II, who entered my consciousness — while I was still an atheist — on the day he sustained a gunshot wound in St. Peter's Square.

In the summer of 1982, I began to meet with a priest to explore my questions, and very quickly I asked to be received into full communion. He smiled wisely and encouraged me to be patient. He said that there were many things I still needed to learn before making that request and that he would teach me.

Close to my university was the town of Washington, New

Jersey — home of the national shrine of Our Lady of Fátima. To that shrine my priest-instructor took me to see popular religion in all its terrible splendor. And there it was: bad art, gaudy statues, old women clothed in black and clutching rosaries, prayers mumbled before banks of burning candles. What I saw made my Anglican aesthetic sensibilities shiver and my evangelical convictions wonder, "What is this all about?"

In time, and with much effort, I came to understand what it's all about. Such devotion arises from the *sensus fidei*, the supernatural sense of the faith of simple Christians who understand by spiritual instinct what it took centuries for the finest minds in the Church to puzzle out — namely, that an ecclesiology without Mary inevitably leads to a Christology without Christ.

In other words, a doctrine of the Church that does not include a detailed reflection on the unique and indispensable role of Mary in the history of salvation will, in short order and without fail, find itself unable to explain how the death and resurrection of Jesus of Nazareth atones for the sins of the whole world. And this is so because of the extraordinary difficulty we have in understanding, accepting, and applying the reality of the Incarnation — the taking of human flesh by the eternal Son of the Father. This is why Pope St. Leo the Great wrote in the mid-fifth century:

> He who is true God is also true Man. Each nature exercises its own activity, in communion with the other. The Word does what is proper to the Word; the flesh fulfills what is proper to the flesh. One and the same Person — this must be said over and over again — is truly the Son of God and truly the Son of Man. He is God in virtue of the fact that in the beginning was the Word, and the Word was with God, and the Word was God. He is Man in virtue of the fact that the Word was made flesh and dwelt among us.

Those words were written by Pope Leo to Patriarch Flavian of Constantinople, and they were a response to the theological crisis that led to the Council of Chalcedon in 451 — a crisis about the relationship of the human and divine natures in the one Person of our Blessed Savior. A major part of this dispute had been resolved twenty years earlier at the Council of Ephesus, which declared that we can, indeed that we must, call the Blessed Virgin Mary *Theotokos*, the Mother of God; otherwise, we do violence to Christ Himself and separate the unity of the two natures in His Person.

And here we reach a central insight: Everything we affirm about Mary, we affirm for the sake of her Son. Every grace we ascribe to Mary, we ascribe as coming from her Son. Every privilege we acknowledge in Mary, we acknowledge as granted by her Son.

In other words, exalting the Mother does not diminish the Son in any way — anymore than the moon detracts from the sun by reflecting its light. Rather, the moon reflects the light of the sun and magnifies its radiant glory.

With the angel of God, we proclaim the Virgin to be full of grace, and in fulfillment of her prophetic hymn of praise, we do call her blessed. But we do so in order — with Mary — to magnify the Lord and to rejoice in God our Savior.

It is to Catholics a source of great sadness that our devotion to the Mother of God is considered by many to be a stumbling block to the restoration of full, visible communion among all Christians. But this is neither the time nor the place to address this question in all its complexity. For now, allow me to suggest some simple "do's" and "don'ts," which might help us move forward together to fulfill Our Lord's prayer that we all be one.

First the "don'ts."

Don't be dismayed by cultural expressions of the Gospel that are foreign to your own. Garish statues and emotional processions are certainly alien to German and English culture, but that does not make them pagan.

Don't allow abuses and exaggerations to distract you from true teaching. The fact that millions of Christians commit adultery each year does not falsify the Gospel truth about marriage. Likewise, the fact that some Christians get carried away in their devotion to the Mother of God does not falsify the truth about her unique place in the economy of salvation.

Now the "do's."

Do insist upon absolute fidelity to the Word of God in asking about all matters of belief — including belief about the Blessed Virgin Mary. Just be absolutely sure to rely on the Word of God — not upon some commentary on that Word. No theologian's opinion — however well respected he may be — is the Word of God. And no theologian can replace the teaching authority of the Church, which alone is competent to transmit the Gospel authentically and authoritatively.

Do bring your own long experience of Christian prayer, teaching, and service to the conversation with other Christians. But also remember that we are searching together for a way forward, and we must be prepared to listen to and learn from one another.

Finally, do read the testimony of an undivided Church to the place of the Blessed Virgin in the drama of salvation. The writings of the Fathers and Doctors speak to us even now in a privileged way, so listen to Irenaeus of Lyons, Basil, and the Gregorys; to Athanasius and Augustine; to Leo and Gregory — the Greats; to Bernard of Clairvaux and Anselm of Canterbury. We may well find the way forward only by looking back.

In closing, permit me to remind you of a bit of your own history. Before Lenior-Rhyne College, there was Highland Academy and then College. The cornerstone of Highland Academy was laid and dedicated in 1882, on the twenty-fifth of March — the Solemnity of the Annunciation. Since there are no coincidences in God, I take this small sign as a providential link between Lenior-Rhyne College and the all-holy and ever-virgin Mother of God.

Remember that we esteem the Blessed Virgin Mary not

only because she is the *Theotokos* but also because through her faith in and perfect obedience to the Word of God she became the first and greatest disciple of her Son and the pattern of Christian discipleship for all ages.

As we celebrate today the Incarnation of the eternal Word, let us respond to the will of God in our lives as did Mary to the annunciation of the angel: Let it be done unto me according to Your Word. Amen.

CHAPTER 20
Hail Mary
By Rev. Terril D. Littrell

(Editor's note: Dr. Littrell uses a version of the mysteries of the Rosary that is somewhat different from that which is familiar to Catholics, specifically the Glorious Mysteries.)

"Hail Mary!" is usually associated with the Roman Rite of the Christian Church. As part of an act of penance for some sin committed, a confessor might prescribe so many Hail Marys and so many Our Fathers. However, it was neither a pope nor prelate, bishop or priest who first addressed the Blessed Virgin Mary in this manner. She was hailed by God's own special messenger, the archangel Gabriel (see Lk 1:26-28).

As far as we know, there were only three people whom the archangel Gabriel ever visited. The first was Daniel. The purpose was to open up Daniel's understanding, to teach and instruct him (see Dn 8:16, 9:21). The second was the priest Zechariah, in the Temple, hundreds of years later. The purpose was to inform him that his wife would have a child who would be the forerunner of our blessed Lord (see Lk 1:19). The third was Mary, a simple peasant girl and virgin, who was engaged to a man named Joseph.

The archangel Gabriel came from the very presence of God in heaven with the greatest news that was ever told. The Messiah was to be born of her. He begins his salutation, "Hail [Mary], full of grace" (Lk 1:28). These words were the beginning of fifteen different mysteries concerning the life, death, and resurrection of Christ, and the role of Mary, His mother. During the course of the events that followed, Mary speaks to us seven times. There are also seven sorrows associated with the angelic salutation.

There are five Joyful Mysteries: The Annunciation — Humility (Lk 1:28); The Visitation — Love of Neighbor (Lk

1:41); The Nativity — The Spirit of Poverty (Lk 2:7); The Presentation — The Virtue of Obedience (Lk 2:22-28); and The Finding in the Temple — The Virtue of Piety (Lk 2:41-52).

There are five Sorrowful Mysteries: The Agony in the Garden — True Contrition (Mk 14:32-36); The Scourging at the Pillar — Virtue of Purity (Mk 15:15); The Crowning of Thorns — Moral Courage (Mk 15:17); The Carrying of the Cross — The Virtue of Patience (Jn 19:17); and The Crucifixion — Final Perseverance (Lk 23:33).

There are five Glorious Mysteries: The Resurrection — Virtue of Faith (Mk 16:6); The Appearance — Consolation (Mk 16:9-18); The Ascension — Virtue of Hope (Acts 1:8-9); The Descent of the Holy Spirit — the Virtue of Love (Acts 2:4); and the Second Coming of Christ — Eternal Happiness (Acts 1:10-11).

Mary speaks seven times in the Gospels: "How will this [miraculous virginal conception] be, since I do not know man?" (Lk 1:34); "I am the Lord's servant, be it done to me as you have said" (Lk 1:38); "My soul praises the Lord, and my spirit has rejoiced in God, my Savior" (Lk 1:46-47); "all generations shall call me blessed" (Lk 1:48); "Son [Jesus], . . . your father and I have been anxiously searching for you" (Lk 2:48); "They [the multitudes] have no more wine" (Jn 2:3); and "Do whatever he [Jesus] tells you" (Jn 2:5).

The Seven Sorrows of Mary: The Prophecy of Simeon (Lk 2:35); The Flight into Egypt (Mt 2:13); Search for the Child Jesus in Jerusalem (Lk 2:48); Meeting Christ on His Way to the Cross (Jn 19:17); Standing at the Foot of the Cross (Jn 19:25); The Descent from the Cross (Jn 19:38); and Assisting at the Burial of Christ (Lk 23:55).

I preached my first sermon, entitled "Hail Mary," on November 30, 1986, at the Ridgedale United Methodist Church in Chattanooga, Tennessee. Many people came to me and said that they would like for me to give the supporting Scriptures for the fifteen mysteries that began with the "Hail

Mary" salutation, the seven words of Mary, and the seven sorrows of Mary. I never dreamt that this service, in honor of our Blessed Mother, would be so popular. Hearts were touched! We give all the glory to God through Jesus Christ, Our Lord. Amen.

CHAPTER 21

The Rosary: Its Origin and Modern Usage

By Margaret O'Connell

Human beings have used and continue to use counters — seeds, pods, rocks, sticks, and beads — to keep count of prayers said, regardless of their faith. So in one sense it might be said that the use of rosary-type "prayer counters" is as old as the human race. But in another and far more important sense, the development of what we call the Rosary is specifically Catholic.

The early Christian ascetics in the Egyptian desert used pebbles to keep count of their prayers, throwing one pebble away for each prayer said. Christian Indians used a similar method to keep track of their prayers when they were captured by pagan countrymen here in North America. In fact, a Rosary ring can be seen at the Martyrs' Shrine in Auriesville, New York. But pebbles are not the most convenient or most portable means of keeping count. On an island at the very edge of the then-known world, monks found a better way to keep count of prayers.

After the fall of Rome, Catholics were divided into those who spoke, read, and wrote Latin, chiefly the clergy, and those not only innocent of Latin but who could not read in their own language. It was this latter group that not only formed the majority of Catholics but that also desired to unite with the clergy in the recitation of the Divine Office (Liturgy of the Hours). And it is to Irish monks that we owe the solution to this problem. Each day's Divine Office contained the one hundred fifty Psalms of David. Irish monks substituted one hundred fifty Paternosters ("Our Fathers") for these Psalms, divided them into three groups of fifty, and suggested the use of hollowed-out seeds or strung pods on a rope to keep count.

So close was the identification between the Divine Office and this Psalter of Paternosters that among lay brothers and some of the laity the opening prayers of the Divine Office, the physical gestures, and the doxology ("Glory Be") were incorporated into the Psalter of Paternosters. The beads were called paternosters or paternoster beads. Use of this Psalter can be dated to A.D. 800 in monasteries and A.D. 1040 among the laity.

The substitution of one hundred fifty "angelic salutations" for one hundred fifty Our Fathers and the development of the Mary Psalter dates at least from the twelfth century. (The "angelic salutation" developed into this prayer: "Hail, Mary, full of grace, the Lord is with thee. Blessed art thou among women and blessed is the fruit of thy womb, Jesus. Amen." The second half, "Holy Mary, Mother of God, pray for us sinners, now and at the hour of our death," was added later.) Again, it was the ignorance of the majority of people that necessitated a pictorial means of teaching Mary's role in our redemption. From the Mary plays enacted during Masses on her feast days came crude pictorial representations in manuscripts (later books) of the events of her life. With the approval of what might be called the primitive Hail Mary as an official prayer of the Church at the end of the twelfth century, people began combining the recitation of the Hail Mary with viewing these pictures. The literate even wrote collections of one hundred fifty praises of Mary, one for each bead.

Note the link with the Divine Office, again: one hundred fifty Psalms, one hundred fifty praises of Mary, one hundred fifty beads. Such primitive Rosaries had to be read and prayed at the same time.

Over time the Paternoster Psalter and the Mary Psalter were combined. The use of paternosters was dropped, except at the beginning of each group of fifty, but the borrowings from the Divine Office (opening prayers, physical gestures, doxology) continued. A legend related in a fourteenth-century manuscript even has Mary telling a monk to say his first fifty in honor of the joy she experienced at the time of the Annunciation, and so on for the other hundred (sorrowful, glorious).

By the end of the fourteenth century, the Carthusians had definitely broken each fifty into five groups of ten with each ten (decade) preceded by an Our Father. And with the publication of the revised Roman Breviary (Divine Office) of 1568, the Hail Mary as we know it came into widespread use.

Still, the Rosary had a way to go. The Irish monks had given the Rosary its basic form and the Carthusians had divided it into fifteen groups of ten with each group preceded by an Our Father. St. Dominic and his followers had propagated this form of prayer. It was then that the Jesuits, beginning with St. Peter Canisius (1521-1597), developed and stressed the importance of the meditative aspects of the Rosary familiar to us today. They were the first, as far as we can tell, to teach that the principal virtue of each mystery should be applied to daily life. Or, as the concluding prayer for the Rosary puts it: "O God, Whose only begotten Son by His life, death, and resurrection, hath purchased for us the rewards of eternal salvation, grant, we pray, that meditating upon these mysteries of the most holy Rosary of the Blessed Virgin Mary, we may imitate what they contain and obtain what they promise."

Until the Second Vatican Council, the Rosary continued admirably to substitute for the Divine Office among the laity. It was our school of meditation on the truths of our faith and the lives of Jesus and Mary. It was the means by which we went to Jesus through Mary. Since the Second Vatican Council, the Liturgy of the Hours (as the Divine Office is now called) is available not only in the vernacular but also in shortened editions well suited to the needs of busy people. And certainly, next to the Holy Sacrifice of the Mass, the Liturgy of the Hours is the best liturgical prayer that could be offered to God. So the question arises: Is the Rosary relevant or useful today? Is it still a school of devotion and learning accessible to everyone?

The Rosary can be rushed. It can be boring to the point of tears or boring to the point of sleep. It can also be the road to unlimited distractions. But these don't have to exist.

The remedy: Apply Luke for the Infancy narratives of the Joyful Mysteries, the Synoptic Gospels for the Sorrowful Mysteries and part of the Glorious Mysteries, and our own well-read and imaginative minds for the last two Glorious Mysteries.

Read about that fateful night journey across the Kidron Valley to an olive grove shining silver in the moonlight, and what happened in that grove while savoring an Our Father and ten Hail Marys. Collect the whole with a Glory Be. This is better prayer, praise, and petition than a whole five decades said pell-mell.

Or, if you've read and heard the account of the Annunciation enough to know it by heart, perhaps you'd enjoy embroidering on its spartan outlines. Set the known story in hilly Galilee of the Gentiles. Give Mary her Hebrew name. Sketch in details of her appearance; of Gabriel's. Try to imagine what that startled Jewish teenager thought beyond what we are told.

While reporterlike you are covering this fulfillment of God's long-ago promise, your fingers and lips are moving along, praying their Hail Marys.

Better yet, you are neither bored to tears or sleep nor on the slippery slope to distractions. Rushed, rote recitation is impossible too.

Reviewing the origins of the Rosary and explaining ways to use the Rosary as a vehicle to meditation and contemplation leave unsaid some hints and some variations that may prove helpful to us during this Marian year.

Maybe it would also be wise to start with a decade a day. That way we "hit-'n'-miss" Rosary types could develop the Rosary habit slowly. We moderns are just too jittery for a crash course in meditation-contemplation if we wish to remain sane and at least no more jittery than usual.

Finally, there are variations on the familiar Rosary that someday you might want to try.

One, from the East, substitutes the Jesus Prayer ("Lord Jesus Christ, Son of the Living God, have mercy on me, a sinner") for the Hail Marys, but retains the Our Fathers and Glory Be's.

Another variation, which I mentioned in the development of the Rosary, is the use of only the first half of the Hail Mary (up to "fruit of thy womb, Jesus. Amen") within the familiar Rosary structure. This is the Rosary used by the children of Fátima before the beautiful Lady visited them.

Now that we no longer need the Rosary as a substitute for the Divine Office, it seems wise to use the Rosary to give our good God the greatest honor and praise outside of the Mass and the Liturgy of the Hours that we can, by making an effort to abide with Him while thinking about His Son and the Mother of His Son, and applying their virtues to ourselves.

CHAPTER 22
An Old Prayer for a Modern World
By Rev. Bonaventure Stefun, O.F.M. Conv.

Cardinal John Wright liked to emphasize the simplicity of faith by accentuating the Rosary. In his dramatic fashion, the Cardinal said that the one item he wanted found on his person when he died would be his rosary. Although he was an intellectual, he was pointing out that the deepest aspects of faith were more devotional than doctrinal.

In the same way, Pope John XXIII opened the Second Vatican Council by pleading for renewed fervor rather than for the definitions of new doctrines. He referred to the Rosary as "David's sling," the instrument of faith capable of withstanding the Goliaths of modern problems.

As much as Pope John called for renewal in the Church, his own practice centered on personal renewal. When he was making his annual retreat at the age of sixty-eight, he concluded that he had better prepare for death. The life expectancy for men at that time was sixty-nine, and Cardinal Roncalli decided he had better get as ready as possible. In his preparation, he resolved to improve the basics. For him, that meant increased devotion at Mass, visits to the Blessed Sacrament, and the daily praying of the Rosary.

Ten years after that significant retreat, the Cardinal became the Pope. He lived on in that capacity for nearly five years and died at the age of eighty-two. Each year during his annual retreat, he repeated the same resolution to intensify the basics, and for Pope John, that always included the Rosary.

The Rosary and John XXIII go together rather easily. A far more astonishing association would be to connect the Rosary with Pope Leo XIII, who reigned from 1878 to 1903. He faced disruption of papal lands, the secularization of Germany in the Kulturkampf, and a full gamut of industrial problems.

Pope Leo was a scholar, philosopher, diplomat, historian, and theologian. He had the intellectual capacity to guide the Church through trying times, and he provided erudite answers with eighty-six encyclicals during his twenty-five-year reign. One of the great encyclicals was *Rerum Novarum* (1891), which established the moral basis for organizing labor.

While dealing with these complicated issues, Leo operated from a policy of total honesty. As a result, his critics insisted that he was giving opponents an unfair advantage. That was especially the case when Leo ordered that the Vatican Archives be made accessible to all scholars in 1883. He was convinced that the Church would be able to survive any conflicts or scandals as long as genuine facts were in the open and dealt with honestly in the present.

The basis for all this confidence was Leo's trust in the Rosary. He saw this simple devotion as the sure means to sustain the faith. In encyclicals published in eleven Septembers of his twenty-five years as pope, Leo called on all the faithful to dedicate the month of October to Our Lady of the Rosary.

In *Laetitiae Sanctae,* Pope Leo XIII's encyclical of 1893 commending devotion to the Rosary, the Holy Father wrote that he was "convinced that the Rosary, if devoutly used, is bound to benefit not only the individual but society at large." As the Lion of Rome, he was expected to provide intricate solutions to complicated problems, and he kept coming back to simple basics, especially the Rosary.

Pope Leo's Rosary encyclicals urged the people to gather daily at home as a family, the foundation of society, so that Mary could take them by the safest, surest way to the Savior. Erudite Leo XIII sounded like simple John XXIII when he insisted in the encyclical of 1894 that the devotion of the Rosary was the best way to keep Jesus uppermost in people's hearts.

The Pontiff wrote that the mysteries of the Rosary appeared "less as truths or doctrines to be speculated upon, than as present facts to be seen and understood." The attachment of a mother's heart had more value than a scholar's perception. When trusting a mother, the encyclical insisted, no disciple could take the wrong turns in following the Master.

That applied to people of all ages, and that was why Pope Leo presented the Rosary as a family devotion. The youngest members could benefit from the Rosary's basic stories (as if they were listening to heavenly fairy tales — except, unlike the usual fairy tales, the Rosary stories are true), and the wisest would not be able to exhaust the depths where meditation with Mary would lead.

When many families assembled in church, the Pope wanted them to pray the Rosary with the Eucharist enthroned, demonstrating Mary's goal of leading her children to Christ. He quoted many examples of people in mission lands who did not have the advantage of a resident priest, but who kept their faith resplendent by praying the Rosary together daily.

In the encyclical of 1893, Pope Leo proposed that the lessons of the Rosary be the counterforce to the major inimical influences in society. He first listed the attitudes bringing about a "downgrade movement of society." These, he said, were: "distaste for a simple life of labor, repugnance to suffering of any kind, and forgetfulness of the future life."

For a correct approach to work and a more simple lifestyle, the Pontiff offered the lessons of the Joyful Mysteries of the Rosary. He proclaimed the Holy Family to be an example of dignified human living. Theirs was a life that "was content with little, seeking rather to diminish the number of their wants, rather than to multiply the sources of their wealth." The result of that approach would be "unbroken harmony, mutual respect and love."

In the Sorrowful Mysteries, Pope Leo pictured a brother limp in death and a mother weak with weeping. "Witnessing these examples of fortitude, not with sight but by faith," the Holy Father wrote, "who is there who would not feel his heart grow warm with the desire of imitating them?" With a mother inspiring courage, the crosses of life would generate far less terror for disciples making sincere submission to their human condition.

For the third great struggle in society, Leo XIII pointed out that modern productivity prompted humans to think that paradise could be attained on earth. They expected that all their many desires would be met, and that there was little need to wait for future fulfillment or a joy beyond the present. As a result, they missed the great joy of heaven, the loving union with the Father.

For Leo XIII, the first of the great modern popes, Mary was the essential example every disciple needed. Her lesson of total faith and lowliness in cooperation with God was the heart of genuine discipleship. The Pope concluded that the devotion of the Rosary was the best aid in developing those traits of discipleship.

Pope Leo XIII wrote eleven official letters, or encyclicals, to demonstrate his conviction concerning the Rosary. The one for 1892 was called *Magnae Dei Matris* ("The Great Mother of God"). In it, he insisted that those who lessened their relationship with Mary weakened their entire faith.

Fifty years later, the Jesuit theologian Father Karl Rahner expressed the same sentiment by saying that devotion to Mary was the very test of faith. Only someone who comprehended her human cooperation with God could recognize the magnificence of His intervention in human salvation.

In that encyclical of 1892, Pope Leo concluded: "In places, families, and nations in which the Rosary of Mary retains its ancient honor, the loss of faith through ignorance and error need never be feared." The devotion of the Rosary is as uncomplicated, and is as equally majestic, as faith itself.

CHAPTER 23

The Power of the Rosary

By Dr. Kevin Orlin Johnson

(Editor's note: This is condensed from *Rosary: Mysteries, Meditations, and the Telling of the Beads*.)

"When you greet me with the angelic salutation," Mary reportedly told St. Eulalia of Spain in the fourth century, "I experience a great thrill of joy." That salutation, "Hail, Mary, full of grace," is the basic vocal prayer of the Rosary. As St. Eulalia herself did before the Virgin corrected her — zipping through them quickly and thoughtlessly — we might take that prayer for granted. But, as the basis of the Rosary, vocal prayers such as the Hail Mary combine into a powerfully effective weapon against what ails us today.

You sometimes hear objections to the Rosary because people think that Matthew 6:7 says that we shouldn't repeat prayers. But this just warns against confusing quantity with quality. Christ spent whole nights in prayer, and He repeated what He said time and again (see Mt 26:44). Besides, He gave us the Our Father as a pattern, and then He repeated it Himself — compare Matthew 6:6-13 and Luke 11:1-4, which happened on another occasion altogether. He even said outright that repeated prayers work beyond the claims of justice (see Lk 11:5-10; 18:1-8; Jas 5:16-17).

So, if you're saying a vocal prayer right, you can't say it often enough; and if you're saying it wrong, it doesn't matter how often you say it — how can you expect God to listen to you, St. Cyprian asked, if you're not even listening to yourself?

But, in praying the Rosary, you don't repeat the vocal prayers just for their own sake. You repeat them as a way to achieve a state of clear meditation, a lively regard of God or of some aspect of God. "To recite the Our Father or the Hail Mary is vocal prayer," St. Teresa of Ávila said in her *Way of Perfec-*

tion. "But behold what poor music you produce when you do this without mental prayer" — what we usually call *meditative prayer.*

It's really the opposite of Oriental meditation, which is thinking about nothing, simply emptying the mind of all conscious thought. Christian meditative prayer is thinking about something, about God or something related to God. The Rosary focuses on each of fifteen episodes in the life of Christ and Mary, the "mysteries" marked off by the decades consisting of one Our Father and ten Hail Marys. Without these meditations, Pope Paul VI reminded us, "the Rosary is a body without a soul, and its recitation is in danger of becoming a mechanical repetition of formulas" (*Marialis Cultus*, Apostolic Exhortation on Devotion to the Blessed Virgin Mary).

Christian meditative prayer begins with *preparation*, which means solitude, silence, and recollection — the remembrance of the presence of God. Then there are the acts of meditation themselves. *Reflections* are the acts of turning the mystery over in your mind, analyzing it, and seeing how each part of it relates to prophecy and to events yet to come in the Gospels and the Acts of the Apostles. You can use pictures or statues of the mystery to help you concentrate, directing your reflections to the mystery, as St. John of the Cross said in the *Ascent of Mount Carmel*, spiritually toward the mystery in "immediate forgetfulness" of the image.

However you do it, you have to make your mind focus on the mystery that you want to meditate about: "The soul is ruined and dissolute when it lets the mind and its thoughts flutter around carelessly. . . . When at last they come straggling home, they drag behind them an even greater burden of desire and greed," Francisco de Osuna warned.

You have to train your natural faculties, such as your *imagination* — talk to Christ as if He were before your bodily eyes. The *Spiritual Exercises* of St. Ignatius of Loyola outline classic ways to harness your imagination as a tool for meditative prayer, but there are countless others.

Memory lets you draw on the fund of information that you've stored up about the mysteries and about your past life. *Reason* gets you past the emotions involved in meditative prayer, a necessary step, but one that's often overlooked.

People naturally feel captivated when they meditate on the Joyful Mysteries, and elated when they think about the Glorious Mysteries. Some weep when they reflect on the Sorrowful Mysteries, and they might take this as a sign of contrition for sin; but interestingly enough, it probably isn't. "A thousand times they will be led to think they weep for God, but they will not be doing so," St. Teresa of Ávila admonishes us in her *Interior Castle*. Pursued for their own sake, these emotions can be an insurmountable roadblock to spiritual growth.

But honest reflection on a mystery goes beyond the examination of that great truth in itself to the examination of truth in yourself. It's like a reflection in a mirror, St. Bernard said that it lets you see the dirt on your face, and it lets you make sure that you've washed it off. Reflection lets you see if your conduct and your will conform to the mystery, and it lets you search for ways to align yourself with it better.

In other words, meditative prayer should end in *resolutions*, promises that you make to yourself and to God to fix the things you've found wanting in yourself. Some teachers compare meditation to the needle and resolutions to the thread — there's no point in meditating without drawing after the prayer those resolutions that mend the soul, and good resolutions aren't much use without meditative prayer.

That's why *petitions* are a necessary part of Christian prayer — "Ask, and it will be given you," Christ said (Mt 7:7), not "You shall receive whether you ask or not." In meditative prayer, you ask for the graces that your examination of conscience indicates that you need, or for any good intention. "Meditation shows us what we need," St. Bernard said, "and petition gets it for us."

The *conclusion* of a session of meditative prayer turns you back into the workaday world, gently, so that you can carry with you the graces that you've received, using them to attain the goals of your resolutions. "A person, given a precious liquid in a porcelain vase to carry home, walks with great care," St. Francis de Sales advised his friend Philothea. "He . . . looks first of all straight ahead for fear of stumbling . . . and secondly at the vase to be sure that it doesn't spill."

Thank God for having heard you — St. Teresa of Ávila used to apologize for the stench that Christ had to endure whenever she approached Him; offer yourself to Him, she would advise, and then get to work.

Resolutions taken in prayer and practiced in life add up to *conversion*. It is virtually impossible that people who have the habit of meditative prayer should be unjust in their dealings with others or with God. "Meditation and sin cannot exist together," St. Alphonsus of Liguori used to say. In fact, Pope St. Pius V remarked that the greatest benefit of the Rosary is that "with the spread of this devotion . . . the faithful . . . have suddenly become different people."

Well, it's not always sudden; it often takes years. But the Rosary, faithfully prayed and well, does work to individual conversion, and enough of those tip the scales for the nation as a whole. That's why Pope Leo XIII could say, "We are convinced that the Rosary, if devoutly used, is bound to benefit not only the individual person but society at large" (*Laetitiae Sanctae*).

In times like ours, who can afford to ignore the power of the Rosary, the Church's great "weapon," as Blessed Padre Pio used to call it. Weapon, indeed. Ferdinand Foch, commander of the French forces in World War I, never failed to pray the Rosary for a single day, even during the most terrible times of battle. It sustained him, and, he said, he often saw Mary's intercession in the strategies that he chose. "Take the advice of an old soldier," he said; "do not neglect praying the Rosary for any reason."

CHAPTER 24
A Gift Rediscovered
By Sister Madeleine Grace, C.V.I.

The Immaculate Conception holds a special place in the history of Catholicism in the United States. In celebration of this great event, the National Shrine of the Immaculate Conception in Washington is a reminder that this land has been dedicated to Mary. However, the historical roots surrounding this feast, both in America and within the Church as a whole, remain somewhat unknown to most Catholics. A few illustrations point to an early devotion in this country to Mary in her Immaculate Conception.

How many American-born Catholics know that the "Father of Waters," the Mississippi River, was originally named the river of Mary Immaculate by Père Marquette? When the missionary set out on his voyage in 1674, he recorded:

> Above all, I placed our voyage under the protection of the Blessed Virgin Immaculate, promising her that, if she granted us the favor of discovering the great river, I would give it the name of the Conception, and that I would also make the first mission that I would establish among those new peoples bear the same name. This I have actually done, among the Illinois.
>
> — Jacques Marquette, "Voyages of Marquette" in *The Jesuit Relations* (Ann Arbor, Michigan: University Microfilms, Inc., 1966, Vol. 59, p. 93)

In fact, as this same story in *The Jesuit Relations* points out, Marquette maintained a dialogue with Mary Immaculate throughout his journey. He wrote in his journal that the Blessed Virgin took care of those on the voyage during the winter months as they never lacked supplies. In his travels, he gave the name of the Immaculate Conception to one of the missions, as he had promised. After his death at the age of thirty-eight, one of his companions remarked that Marquette had an extraordinary devotion to Mary in her Immaculate Conception:

> But that which apparently predominated was a devotion, altogether rare and singular, to the Blessed Virgin, and particularly toward the mystery of her Immaculate Conception. It was a pleasure to hear him speak or preach on that subject. All his conversations and letters contained something about the Blessed Virgin Immaculate — for so he always called her.
> — "Voyages of Marquette," p. 207

Prior to that event, some of the earliest American Catholic colonists, arriving on the shores of Maryland in 1634, consecrated the colony they were about to establish to the Immaculate Conception (see *Behold Your Mother, Woman of Faith: A Pastoral Letter on the Blessed Virgin Mary,* National Conference of Catholic Bishops [Washington, D.C.: U.S. Catholic Conference], 1973, p. 54). The oldest church in the Americas dedicated to the Immaculate Conception was built in 1666 in Quebec. Another church was built in honor of Mary's Immaculate Conception at the Prairie de Magdalen in Louisiana in 1675 (see Ralph J. Ohlmann, "The Immaculate Conception and the United States," in *The Promised Woman: An Anthology of the Immaculate Conception,* edited by Stanley G. Mathews [St. Meinrad, Indiana: Grail], 1954, p. 90).

Mary has been venerated in the Americas ever since early colonial history. When Columbus sailed to this land in the *Santa María,* he named the second island he sighted Santa María de la Concepción. (It was only fitting that he named the first after the Savior: San Salvador.)

Thus, history reveals that the Immaculate Conception was celebrated on American soil centuries before the official promulgation by the Church. Yet, how did the Church arrive at its promulgation, since the terms themselves are not recorded in the scriptural account of Mary's life?

Pope Pius IX, in the document *Ineffabilis Deus* (1854), referred to scriptural passages that imply the belief. The early Church Fathers looked upon Mary as the Second Eve. This comparison is born out in Genesis 3:15 of the *Douay-Rheims* version of the Bible: "I will put enmities between thee and the woman, and thy seed and her seed." Strictly speaking, "woman" in the passage refers to Eve; however, considering the Eve-Mary comparison, the woman is seen as Mary. Her seed is normally interpreted as the Messiah. The serpent is the demon. The enmity ends with the crushing of the demon and the reestablishing of God's rights in the eschatological world to come. If one reads the remainder of that verse, the author points out that this woman strikes the serpent's head with her foot. Thus, Mary, through Jesus, has triumphed over evil (see Pius IX, "*Ineffabilis Deus,*" in *Papal Documents on Mary* [Milwaukee: Bruce, 1954], pp. 17-18).

In his document, Pius IX likewise noted the account of the Annunciation, during which Gabriel addresses Mary as "full of grace," as pointing to the privilege of the Immaculate Conception. Although his commentary does not delve into the Greek origins of the phrase "Hail, full of grace," these words do imply an unvarying continuity in Greek. One could determine from the Greek that because of the grace Mary has received, no other human being can be compared to Mary in holiness (see Aidan Carr and German Williams, "Mary's Immaculate Conception," *Mariology,* 1, edited by Juniper Carol [Milwaukee: Bruce, 1954], p. 339). Similarly, the Pontiff pointed out that the early Church Fathers looked upon Mary as "an almost infinite treasury, an inexhaustible abyss of these gifts [of the Holy Spirit], to such an extent that she was never subject to the curse and is together with her Son the only partaker of perpetual benediction" (*Ineffabilis Deus*, No. 19). Thus, within the narrative of the Visitation, she was worthy to hear the exclamation of Elizabeth: "Blessed art thou among women, and blessed is the fruit of thy womb" (Lk 1:42, *Douay-Rheims*).

The Pope, in *Ineffabilis Deus*, extended his study beyond

that of Scripture to the writers of the early Church. One finds great esteem for Mary within the writings of these authors. The pontiff highlighted the terms immaculate, spotless, and innocent as applied to Mary by these Church Fathers. The document reaches its culmination in the definition of the teaching of the Immaculate Conception:

> Mary in the first instant of her conception, by a singular grace and privilege granted by almighty God, in view of the merits of Jesus Christ, the Savior of the human race, was preserved free from all stain of original sin, is a doctrine revealed by God and therefore to be believed firmly and constantly by all the faithful.
> — *Ineffabilis Deus*, No. 25

One might determine from the familiarity of the teaching that this doctrine was easily derived. However, the lateness of the proclamation in Church history provides a clue that the proclamation of the Immaculate Conception in 1854 followed centuries of dispute over the topic.

Perhaps the clearest reference in this early period to the Immaculate Conception is found in the sermons of John of Damascus, a Greek theologian who lived from about 675 to 749. John saw the pregnancy and birth of the child of Anne as an end to mystical barrenness. "Anne . . . gave birth to a child, whose equal had never been created and never can be" (St. John Damascene, "On the Crowning of Our Lady," in *St. John Damascene on Holy Images followed by Three Sermons on the Assumption,* translated by Mary H. Allies [London: Thomas Baker, 1898], p. 156). John, in referring to the Annunciation account, pointed out that Mary was worthy of grace and found it. He tells us:

> She found grace who had done the deeds of grace, and had reaped its fullness. She found grace who brought forth the source of grace, and was a rich harvest of grace.

She found an abyss of grace who kept undefiled her double virginity, her virginal soul no less spotless than her body; hence her perfect virginity.

> — "On the Crowning of Our Lady," p. 158

The Scholastic age witnessed a great deal of debate on belief in the Immaculate Conception. A significant defense of the Immaculate Conception came from Eadmer (d. 1124), an English historian, theologian, and member of the household of St. Anselm of Canterbury. In his treatise, "The Conception of the Blessed Virgin," he held that Mary was free from original sin due to her dignity as Mother of the Redeemer and also mistress and empress of heaven and earth. Eadmer saw as pivotal to the Immaculate Conception Mary's cooperation with her Son in His role of redemption. The Immaculate Conception could have taken place even though Mary was not born from a virgin because Christ willed it:

> If God gives the chestnut the possibility of being conceived, nourished and formed under thorns, but remote from them, could He not grant to the human body which He was preparing for Himself to be a temple in which He would dwell bodily . . . that although she was conceived among the thorns of sin, she might be rendered completely immune from their pricks? He could do it; if, therefore, He willed it, He did it.
>
> — Eadmer, "The Conception of the Blessed Virgin," as quoted in Hilda Graef's *Mary: A History of Doctrine and Devotion* (New York: Sheed and Ward, 1963, Vol. 1, p. 220)

While the relationship of concupiscence to sin had been a major difficulty during this period, the main objection to the teaching during this era was that the idea was incompatible with the universality of the Redemption.

John Duns Scotus (c. 1265-1308), *Doctor Marianus,* or

the "Marian Doctor," broke the impasse with his own acceptance of the Immaculate Conception. Duns Scotus pointed out that a Redeemer who preserves from sin is more perfect than one who frees from sin. There was already general acceptance that Mary was free from actual sin. This Redeemer prevented original sin as a more perfect and direct act than preventing actual sin (see Duns Scotus, "Opus Parisiense," in *Theologiae Marianae Elementa,* edited by Carolus Balic [Sibenici: Kacic, 1933], L. III. dist. 3, Qu. I). This change of stance in theology became very influential in later theological writing.

After the time of Duns Scotus, the debate over the Immaculate Conception reached a feverish pitch at intervals but gradually moved toward a greater acceptance. For the entire Church, Pope Innocent XII (*In Excelsa*, 1695) provided for the Office and Mass of the Conception of the Immaculate Virgin Mary, and Pope Clement XI (*Commissi Nobis*) established the holy day of obligation in 1708 (see Michael O'Carroll, "Immaculate Conception," in *Theotokos: A Theological Encyclopedia of the Blessed Virgin Mary* [Wilmington, Delaware: Michael Glazier, 1986], pp. 181-82).

Within modern times, John Henry Newman (1801-1890) expressed his approval of the doctrine only five years before it was officially proclaimed. In one of his sermons on Mary in the year 1849, the convert to Catholicism referred to the teaching of the early Church Fathers that Mary is the Second Eve:

> It was a season of grace and prodigy, and these were to be exhibited in a special manner in the person of His Mother. The course of ages was to be reversed; the tradition of evil was to be broken; a gate of light was to be opened amid the darkness, for the coming of the Just; — a Virgin conceived and bore Him. It was fitting, for His honor and glory that she, who was the instrument of His bodily presence, should first be a miracle of His grace; it was fitting that she should triumph, where Eve

had failed, and should "bruise the serpent's head": by the
spotlessness of her sanctity.

— John Henry Newman, *Discourses Addressed to Mixed Congregations* (London: Burns, Oates, and Co., 1871, pp. 354-355)

In corresponding with his confrere Edward B. Pusey, Newman pointed out that Mary has been called the Second Eve by the early Church Fathers. Since Eve received the supernatural gift of grace from the moment of her existence, how could one deny that Mary did not have that gift? Newman wrote to Pusey that he found the doctrine of the Immaculate Conception bound up in the doctrine of the early Fathers, that Mary is the Second Eve (see Hilda Graef, *God and Myself: The Spirituality of John Henry Newman* [New York: Hawthorn Books, 1968], p. 170).

A heightened interest in Marian devotion in the nineteenth century and an increase in support for this teaching can be found in the revelations to Catherine Labouré in the Rue-du-Bac in Paris in the year 1830, and the apparitions at Lourdes in 1858. In Paris, the Blessed Virgin commissioned a Daughter of Charity, Catherine Labouré, to have made what is now known as the Miraculous Medal, with these words: "O Mary, conceived without sin, pray for us who have recourse to thee." The popularity of the medal spurred a prayer movement in honor of the Immaculate Conception (see Omer Englebert, *Catherine Labouré and the Modern Apparitions of Our Lady,* translated by Alastair Guinav [New York: P. J. Kenedy and Sons, 1959], p. 40). The apparitions at Lourdes during which Mary proclaimed to Bernadette Soubirous, "I am the Immaculate Conception," took place four years after the papal announcement. The popularity of the shrine at Lourdes is evident today in the number of pilgrims. Of all the Marian shrines in the world, it today holds the widest international appeal (see Michael O'Carroll, "Lourdes," in *Theotokos: A Theological Encyclopedia of the Blessed Virgin Mary,* p. 224).

About the same time that these events were occurring, the American bishops at their sixth Provincial Council in Baltimore (1864), proclaimed Mary immaculately conceived as the Patroness of the United States and requested that the Holy Father confirm this choice. In 1866, the American hierarchy petitioned Rome that the Feast of the Immaculate Conception be made a holy day of obligation in this country. That petition was granted two years later (see Ralph J. Ohlmann, "The Immaculate Conception and the United States," in *The Promised Woman: An Anthology of the Immaculate Conception,* pp. 92-94).

One might look upon the gift of the Immaculate Conception to the Mother of God as creating a distance between Mary and the faithful. The American Catholic bishops reminded all that "her privileged origin is the final step in preparing mankind to receive the Redeemer" (*Behold Your Mother, Woman of Faith: A Pastoral Letter on the Blessed Virgin Mary,* p. 56).

Thus, this gift means that "God surrounds the life of man with redemptive love, [and] . . . with loving fidelity" (Karl Rahner, *Mary, Mother of the Lord: Theological Meditations* [New York: Herder and Herder, 1963], pp. 44-47).

Rahner goes on to inform us that in Mary and her Immaculate Conception it is clear that the eternal mercy of God has "enveloped man" from the beginning. Certainly, then, the Immaculate Conception is a steppingstone to union with the Son.

The majestic structure of the National Shrine of the Immaculate Conception reminds Americans that their Catholic heritage calls them to search more deeply into this Marian event, to find that the privilege of the Immaculate Conception becomes a gift to all as the gateway to redemption.

There is much to be drawn from the life of a French missionary looking out on an unknown terrain and foreign people and seeking the intercession of Mary in her Immaculate Conception. Marquette's dialogue with Mary led him to the Savior. It is this continuous dialogue with Mary in the lives of the faithful that can lead to the immediate union with her Son.

CHAPTER 25

Marian Year: Ushering in a New Era of Peace

By Rev. Giles Dimock, O.P.

Though only a youngster in 1954, I have vivid memories of the Marian year called by Pope Pius XII to commemorate the one hundredth anniversary of the promulgation of the doctrine of the Immaculate Conception of the Blessed Virgin Mary.

I can still remember walking through the little nineteenth-century fishing village that was my home, delivering papers. Halfway through my route I would stop at the parish church, enter its shadowy interior gilded with the light of the setting sun streaming through its stained-glass windows. I would drop to my knees before the altar and pray before the hand-carved crucifix that my great-great grandfather had brought from Portugal and presented to the church. Then I would go to Our Lady's altar and pray the prayer that Pope Pius XII had composed for the occasion with its beautiful quotation from the Book of Judith applied to Our Lady: "You are the glory of Jerusalem, the joy of Israel; you are the fairest honor of our race." Refreshed by my visit, I would continue on my paper route.

On New Year's Day 1987, amidst the splendor and glitter of the solemn liturgy at St. Peter's, Pope John Paul II, who often catches us all by surprise, announced that he was proclaiming a new Marian year, not as a memorial of a past event but to prepare us for the new millennium that will begin at the turn of the century. As he said, ". . . We desire, O Mary, that you shine on the horizon of the advent of our times, as we approach the third millennium after Christ. We desire to deepen our awareness of your presence in the mystery of Christ as the Council taught."

The Pope, in proclaiming the Marian year that began on Pentecost Sunday in 1987 and ended on the feast of the Assumption of Our Lady the following year, proposed Mary as the model for Christians because of her example of utter conformity to God's will as the Handmaid of the Lord at Nazareth, at Bethlehem, and on Calvary. Our present world — which especially during this last century has wanted "to come of age" (that is, be a law unto itself, be completely autonomous) — needs to rediscover how to say "yes" to God and thus let Him be Lord of its destiny.

Perhaps this is why, during the past century and a half, God has sent Mary as a prophetess — a messenger — to call us to Himself by way of conversion, prayer, and penance. These notes were first sounded in Paris, when she appeared to St. Catherine Labouré, anticipating these same guidelines she offered at Lourdes, which were made more explicit at Fátima. Here Our Lady predicted World War II, the spread of Communism and worse if humanity did not turn to God and, yet, provided the means to do so: saying the Rosary and meditating on the mysteries of the life, death, and resurrection of her Son; the offering of the crosses of daily life as a sacrifice to God; and the consecration of the world and each of us to her Immaculate Heart so that through her intercession, our hearts might become more like hers — totally focused on Jesus. She predicted that her heart would triumph and usher in a new era of peace.

Note how all of these apparitions underscore the basic Gospel message of prayer and conversion. In the light of this basic Marian message to return to Gospel values, we can see why our Holy Father, the supreme pastor of the Church, directs us to look to Mary as embodying the memory of the Church.

The Church with Mary rejoices in the good and at the same time weeps over the tragedy of the human race: "How many hopes, yet how many threats, how many joys, yet how many sufferings . . . what great sufferings! We must all, as a Church, treasure and meditate on these events in our hearts. Just like the Mother, we must ever learn more from you, O Mary, how to be Church in the passing of the millennium."

To learn to be Church for the new era will mean becoming those handmaids and servants of the Lord, responding to

His Word in serenity and peace. It also means being converted or turning our backs on sin and doing penance or reparation for our own personal sin. Pope Pius XII warned that the modern world had lost its sense of sin and our present Pontiff has reiterated the same theme in his encyclical "Reconciliation and Penance." In that document he reminds us that we need to make satisfaction for our sins, as Pope Paul VI had said before him in the "Apostolic Constitution on Indulgences."

Further, the holiness of the moral order needs to be recognized, as well as the majesty of God's glory that sin has obliterated. Even when our sins are forgiven, God's justice must be redressed and the imbalance our sins have caused be restored, in purgatory hereafter or in the sufferings of our present life.

Yet Pope Paul VI reminds us that in this we are not alone, that we are surrounded by the infinite merits of Jesus Christ, and by the prayers and merits of our brothers and sisters, the saints recognized by the Church, and above all, Our Lady, the Immaculate One. These superabundant graces the Church shares in the communion of saints by applying the fruits of the redemption won by Christ in Himself and in His saints to those of us who need them.

With Mary, we as Church will remember the sufferings and sins of humanity, our own included, and we will heed Our Lady's call to penance and reparation, thus preparing for the new millennium of the Lord, the one in which her heart will triumph, the one looked forward to so confidently by Pope John Paul II in his encyclical "Redeemer of Man," issued at the beginning of his reign. All we must do is respond in prayer and penance.

CHAPTER 26
The Apparitions at Guadalupe
By Catherine M. Odell

For fifty-seven years, Juan Diego had been living near the shore of Lake Texcoco in a village hugging Tlatelolco, the Aztec capital. As he walked toward Tlatelolco on a chilly morning in 1531, his thoughts returned to the years of Aztec pagan rites and despicable human sacrifice. Later, the Spanish conquistadors had overwhelmed the Aztec chieftains who ruthlessly ruled the Indian tribes. For Juan and fifteen million Indians, a new time and spirit then began in his homeland.

In Juan's own mind, only the last six of his years had been truly joyful. In 1525, he and his wife, Maria Lucia, had been baptized as Christians. On most days, well before dawn, Juan was somewhere on this road, headed to or from Mass. He lived in the village of Tolpetlac, near Cuauhtitlan. This day, December 9, 1531, was a Saturday, a day on which a special Mass was said in honor of the Virgin Mary.

For some time, his early morning walks had been solitary when he crossed the hill of Tepeyac and the Tepeyac causeway to Tlatelolco, the future Mexico City. Juan's wife had died. There was only his uncle Juan Bernardino. Juan Diego thought of his dead Maria Lucia many times as he made his way. There had been no children, and she had been precious to him.

As Juan approached the crest of Tepeyac Hill, he saw a cloud encircled with a rainbow of colors. Then he heard strange music coming from the hill as well. Could it be from some kind of rare bird, he wondered? He stared up at the hill and the sun now rising behind it. A woman's voice was calling above the music. He was fascinated but confused.

"Juanito, Juan Dieguito . . ." the voice came, urging him. Since it seemed to be coming from behind the top of the hill, he ascended to the crest to look. A young woman, strikingly beautiful, stood there beckoning him. She radiated such light and joy that Juan Diego could think of nothing more to do than drop to his knees and smile at her.

Everything around her seemed to catch the sweet fire she glowed with. The leaves of the plants surrounding her on the hill were aglow; the branches of the trees and bushes shone like polished gold. Around the whole hill a rainbow of multi-colored light seemed to have descended.

"Juanito [Little John], my sweet child, where are you going?" the woman asked him in Nahuatl, his own tongue.

"My Lady and my child," he replied in an Indian idiom of endearment, "I am on my way to the church at Tlatelolco to hear Mass."

Then, with no further introduction, the shining young woman spoke very seriously and yet lovingly to Juan Diego. He listened with an intensity born of instant devotion. The woman was so beautiful, so gracious, he could not do otherwise.

"You must know and be very certain in your heart, my son," she began, "that I am truly the perpetual and perfect Virgin Mary, holy Mother of the true God through whom everything lives, the Creator and Master of heaven and earth.

"I wish and intensely desire that in this place my sanctuary be erected so that in it I may show and make known and give all my love, my compassion, my help, and my protection to the people. I am your merciful Mother, the Mother of all of you who live united in this land, and of all mankind, of all those who love me, of those who cry to me, of those who seek me, of those who have confidence in me. Here I will hear their weeping, their sorrow, and will remedy and alleviate their suffering, necessities, and misfortunes.

"And so that my intentions may be made known, you must go to the house of the bishop of Mexico and tell him that I sent you and that it is my desire to have a sanctuary built here."

Overwhelmed at knowing the identity of this woman, Juan then bowed in obedience to her request. Immediately, and without turning back, he took leave of her and hurried toward the causeway into the city. He knew where to find the house of His Excellency Don Juan de Zumarraga, the recently named bishop of New Spain, as Mexico was called.

Juan rapped on the door of the bishop's house and waited. It was still early morning, shortly after dawn. The bishop's servants opened the door to him with looks of scorn in their eyes: *This Indian! Who was he to think of imposing on the lordly bishop, and at this hour?* But Juan was eventually admitted into the bishop's study.

With patience, the Spanish-born bishop listened as Juan told of his encounter with the Mother of God at the top of Tepeyac Hill, translated by an aide from the Indian's Nahuatl dialect. Bishop Zumarraga was understanding, but he did not really believe Juan's words. Tepeyac, the bishop had learned, was the site of the temple of the Aztec corn goddess, Tonantzin. Perhaps this story was a jumble of that tradition and newfound Christian beliefs the Indian claimed.

The bishop told Juan Diego that he would think over what he had said. "Come back to see me in a few days," he suggested.

Juan Diego was indeed simple-hearted. He had not anticipated that Bishop Zumarraga would doubt him. The image of the Virgin was so sharply and beautifully impressed upon his own spirit. It was hard to believe that anyone else would deny her wishes. Heavyhearted, he headed back to Tepeyac, thinking himself a failure.

As Juan climbed the rise to Tepeyac once again, the Lady was suddenly standing toward the top. He ran closer, dropped to his knees, and dropped his head as well. He was ashamed, but hoped that she would understand that he had tried. With deep regret, he told her of his attempt to convince Bishop Zumarraga and of the bishop's doubting eyes and puzzling smile. This man of God thought that Juan Diego was a liar or a fool.

Burdened by his own littleness, the quiet, good-hearted Indian broke down. Perhaps, he suggested, she could find a more eloquent, more persuasive messenger.

If anything, as Juan Diego later told it, his recitation of failures warmed her smile and her apparent affection for him. Her words were consoling. There were many others she could send, she admitted, but she had chosen him. Her request would be answered through his efforts, she promised.

Courage and self-esteem once again flickered inside him. Taking leave of "my Dear One, my Lady," Juan made his way now to his home. On the following day, Sunday, December 10, he planned to visit the bishop's house once again.

The next day was chilly, and Juan Diego made his way to Mass somewhat later than usual in the morning. His coarse cloak was needed, and he thanked the good God for it as he made his way to Mass. His spirit was at peace concerning the challenge after Mass. The Virgin told him that he would be the one to get her message across to the only man who could have a church built.

At the home of the bishop, Juan's heart was once again thumping wildly with anxiety and fear. This time, Bishop Zumarraga listened more closely. His eyes did not wander all over the Indian's face, looking for a sign of instability or a penchant for lying. He looked straight into Juan's dark eyes as he spoke, with an aide interpreting. Still, when Juan Diego was finished with his story — the same story as the day before — the bishop again refused to commit himself. He needed proof, he said.

"Perhaps you can bring me some sign of the Lady as a tangible proof that she is the Mother of God and that she definitely wants a temple built at Tepeyac Hill," he said. Then Bishop Zumarraga smiled at Juan and left it at that.

Simply and humbly, Juan agreed. But the bishop was thoroughly surprised by the Indian's consent to provide a miracle. As Juan left, Bishop Zumarraga sent two servants after him to track his movements. Outside the city, the men from the bishop's house lost sight of Juan Diego. He seemed to disappear into thin air, or into the sunset settling over the land.

In fact, Juan Diego had again entered that special realm

where his time and space were meshed with the Virgin's on Tepeyac Hill. He greeted her and told her of the bishop's request for proof. Gently, and with a smile, she assured Juan that there would be a sign on the following day.

The bishop would have no more doubts.

If Juan was as happy as a man could be when descending the hill, the joy soon vanished. When he reached home, he found his uncle, his only relative, deathly ill. Juan Bernardino had a soaring fever.

On the following day, Juan Diego could not leave his uncle's side. He was frightened that the old man would die. There seemed to be no break in the fever's grip. Juan Diego's heart was heavy, and heavier still when he thought about his forsaken appointment with the bishop. When he thought of the beautiful Virgin Mother waiting for him to fulfill his promise, he was sick at heart. He almost wished that he too were on his deathbed.

Night brought no relief for Juan Bernardino. The sick man asked his nephew to leave early on the following morning for the monastery of Santiago Tlatelolco. He wished to receive the sacraments of the anointing of the sick and of the Holy Eucharist.

Once he was on the road again, Juan began to fear meeting the Virgin. It was just before dawn on Tuesday, December 12. The day before, he was to have taken the verifying sign to the bishop for "his Dear One, his Lady." How could he tell her that he had failed once again? The most direct route to the monastery would take him near Tepeyac and the shining Mother of God. He decided to take the long way around.

As he was skirting the hilltop where he had seen her, Juan Diego was suddenly face to face again with the heavenly Lady. He shrank with embarrassment, but her greeting dispelled it.

"What troubles you, my dear son? Where are you going?" she asked.

Juan raised his eyes to her then and told her of the illness of his beloved uncle, Juan Bernardino. He had to care for him, he explained; there was no one else to do so. He begged her forgiveness for delaying in the mission she had given him. The Blessed Virgin Mary's response was reassuring:

"Listen and be sure, my dear son, that I will protect you; do not be frightened or grieved or let your heart be dismayed, however great the illness may be that you speak of. Am I not here, I who am your mother, and is not my help a refuge? Am I not of your kind? Do not be concerned about your uncle's illness, for he is not going to die. Be assured, he is already well. Is there anything else that you need?"

With these words, the world of Juan Diego was once again washed with the clear, bright light of hope. Whatever the Virgin had said would surely come to pass. He listened as she gave him instructions about carrying the providential sign to Bishop Zumarraga. He would carry a bouquet of roses, Castilian roses, miraculously flowering on Tepeyac Hill in winter. These he was to take to the bishop.

The Virgin directed him to climb to the top of Tepeyac Hill. He was to pick the roses now growing there where only cactus, thistles, and thornbush had previously been seen. Juan's eyes grew wide at the lush abundance of roses of every color. He began to pluck them in great bunches and carry them back down to the Virgin. She arranged them in his *tilma*.

When it was heavy with the fragrant and radiant roses — heaven's own hybrids — Juan carefully put the folded cloak over his head once again. He tied one corner to the top of the *tilma* at his shoulder to keep the flowers from tumbling out. Then, with a loving smile and farewell to the Lady, he was off again to the bishop's residence. Talk to no one but the bishop, the Virgin had warned Juan. It was the last of four apparitions of the Blessed Virgin to Juan Diego at Guadalupe. He did not realize it as he left her, but Juan would only see the Virgin again in the image she would leave behind.

At the home of Bishop Zumarraga, Juan Diego was admitted for the third time in four days. There was no scorn on the faces of the bishop's servants this time. With open curiosity, they tried to see what be was carrying in the fold of his *tilma*. But Juan only held the ends of the garment closer to his chest, pushing the curious back. The roses were not to be crushed!

When he was in the presence of Bishop Zumarraga this time, Juan bubbled with his message. The bishop stared at the *tilma* he was clutching. He listened as his interpreter struggled to keep up with the unbroken litany of Nahuatl enthusiasm. Juan Diego shared the whole story about his uncle's sickness and his inability to come the day before, about the day's encounter with the Virgin once again, about her insistence that a church be built there on Tepeyac Hill.

Finally, Juan told of the gathering of the roses and of the way the Holy Mother arranged them with care in his cloak. With a smile of the purest joy, Juan then dramatically let loose the bottom of his *tilma*. The roses would fall to the floor in a rainbow cascade of glory at the bishop's feet . . . or so Juan thought.

The bishop did watch as several roses fell to his carpet, but then his eyes moved back up to the *tilma* and filled with tears. He fell speechless to his knees before Juan, who was still wearing the cloak, and began to beg pardon of the Virgin. There on the rough cactus-fiber *tilma* was an exquisite full-length portrait of the Virgin Mother of God, just as Juan had described her.

Now Juan Diego himself looked down at the front of his much-used cloak. Below him was a rendering of the heavenly woman he had so recently seen bending and arranging the roses in his cloak. She had been attired in a dark turquoise mantle just like the figure in this portrait emblazoned on his old *tilma*.

A pink robe adorned the image, just as the Lady had looked at Tepeyac. Her dark black hair could be seen beneath the mantle. Her posture was an attitude of humility and prayer, with the small, delicate hands joined, the head bowed to the left, the dark eyes half shaded by the eyelids. The eyes seemed patient, submissive. The facial features of the Virgin were delicate, beautiful, Indian in character but universal in appeal.

By now, Juan's heart was in his throat, choking him with joy and tears. He started to lift the cloak up over his head, and the bishop quickly rose from his knees to help him with the treasure. After some hesitation, Bishop Zumarraga carried it respectfully to his chapel and laid it before the Blessed Sacrament. By now, his entire household and a number of priests were also gathered around the miraculous portrait. Prayers rose in the chapel as groups of twos and threes spontaneously approached the *tilma* to kiss the bottom of it.

On December 13, the following day, Juan, who had stayed with the bishop overnight, began to trek back to Tepeyac Hill. This time his journey trailed a retinue of believers and the curious. Bishop Zumarraga asked the visionary to take him to see the place where Our Lady had touched New Spain.

Following this, Juan Diego hurried to his home. He had told the bishop about the illness of his uncle but believed, as the Lady had promised, that he would find him well. Juan Bernardino was well. In fact, he was fully recovered and told his nephew that the Virgin had visited him too:

"I too have seen her. She came to me in this very house and spoke to me. She told me too that she wanted a temple to be built at Tepeyac Hill. She said that her image should be called 'Holy Mary of Guadalupe,' though she did not explain why."

Juan de Zumarraga, a man who had left a Franciscan priory to come to this new land, was stirred to his depths. Our Lady of Guadalupe was known to the Spanish as an ancient statue depicting the divine motherhood of the Blessed Virgin.

Some questions were to continue throughout history concerning this name. Some authorities would suggest that Zumarraga and the others heard a Nahuatl word, *Coatalocpia* (pronounced "Cuatlashupe"), which means "Who crushed the Stone Serpent." The serpent beneath the feet of the Virgin on Juan Diego's cloak was a symbol for the Indians. It brought to mind the pagan symbol of their Aztec religion, demanding human sacrifice.

In compliance with the wishes of the Virgin, Bishop Zumarraga planned to have an *hermita*, a little chapel or church, built there by Christmas. In the next two weeks, Indians flocked to Tepeyac Hill to erect the shelter for their Lady. On December 26, 1531, the day after Christmas and precisely two weeks after the miraculous image appeared, a procession was held. With great pomp, the cloak of Juan Diego was carried from the bishop's church to the chapel.

Accounts of the procession say that the Indians of the region had strewn the four-mile route with herbs and flowers. Dressed in bright costumes and adorned with feathers, hundreds danced as the image was borne past. But a tragedy along the way spread the devotion to Our Lady of Guadalupe even more.

As part of the celebration, the Indians reenacted a mock battle by the lake near Tepeyac Hill. In the excitement, one of the Indians was accidentally pierced with an arrow in the neck. He died near the feet of the bishop and others escorting the precious *tilma*.

With grief, but with faith too, he was picked up and placed in front of the mounted image of Our Lady of Guadalupe. Within moments, the "dead" man sat up. The arrow was carefully withdrawn, with no apparent damage except for a scar where the arrow had entered. Tepeyac Hill went wild with joy. Spaniards and the Aztecs, recently released from the horror of a pagan cult, had discovered a living Mother who cared for her children.

To say that the life of Juan Diego was never the same is to state the obvious. He gave the cornfields and the small house that he owned to Juan Bernardino. A small hut was then built for the visionary on Tepeyac Hill. He acted as sacristan at the *hermita*, telling and retelling the story of the apparitions, the blessed *tilma*, and the wonders.

Bishop Zumarraga granted Juan the special permission

to receive the Eucharist at Mass three times a week, an unusual concession in that century. Juan made use of it but never with any sense of superiority or prestige. A major interrogation of natives of the area in 1666 revealed that, in those years following the apparitions, Juan was called "The Pilgrim." Villagers living near Tepeyac recalled that their great-grandparents or grandparents often saw Juan making his way to Mass. He was always alone, always aglow with a special peace and joy.

In 1548, both Juan Diego and Bishop Zumarraga died within a few days of each other. Juan was seventy-four; Bishop Zumarraga died at seventy-two. In the decade following the apparitions and the creation of the Guadalupe image, eight million Indians were baptized, and the growth of Christian conversion and devotion continued throughout the century.

The image of "Holy Mary of Guadalupe" has its mysteries for each century and culture to solve. In the century of its origin, the sixteenth, the picture of the Virgin functioned as a sort of graphic catechism for the Indian culture. In writing, the Aztecs used a form of picture writing similar to the approach of Egyptian hieroglyphics thousands of years earlier.

Here was a beautiful maiden of their own kind. She stood with an attitude of peace and prayer. When they viewed the portrait as a whole, the Indians could see and "read" that this new maiden was more powerful than any and all of their pagan gods, and she did not demand their blood. Her kindness, her care for them, offered them her Son's body and blood instead. Jesus Christ would sustain them; His Mother would be their Mother and Protector.

Added to all this, the Indians could see that the Lady wore a brooch or pin at her throat with a black cross on it. That was the symbol used by the Franciscan friars who had come with the conquistadors early in the century. She was of heaven, and represented heaven's power.

In 1709, a massive basilica was erected at the base of the hill to house the revered image left on Juan Diego's cloak. For over two centuries it drew pilgrims from Mexico and from all over the world. In 1921, a bomb hidden in a bouquet of flowers was placed on the altar just beneath the Guadalupe image. Since 1917, the national constitution had fostered an intensely anti-Catholic rule in Mexico. The bomb went off during Mass and shattered parts of the altar. However, no one attending Mass in the Guadalupe basilica was touched and the *tilma* too was un-harmed.

In 1976, a new Basilica of Our Lady of Guadalupe was dedicated in Mexico City, while the older one was left standing on ground said to be sinking. Processions still bring thousands on their knees to the feet of the Virgin. Scientists of the twentieth century, in a different way, have also had to bow to the image.

Dr. Philip S. Callahan, an infrared specialist, biophysicist, and entomologist for the U.S. Department of Agriculture in Gainesville, Florida, studied the Guadalupe image in the spring of 1979. His work was done on behalf of the "Image of Guadalupe Research Project."

After four hundred forty-eight years, the rough fabric on which the image was imprinted was still then in fine condition. Essentially, the fabric could have been compared to gunnysacking, Callahan said. The pigments that created the image, the researchers discovered, were similar to earth pigments that would have been in use during Juan Diego's lifetime. Their color and quality were still rich, while the painted embellishments added in later decades had begun to fade and crack.

There had been no sizing or preparatory paint laid upon the surface of the fabric. There was no hint of preliminary sketching lines underneath — a shock to those who claimed that the painting was made by human hands. But on close inspection, the golden sunrays, stars, gold trim on the mantle, the moon, and the angel were found to be human "embellishments." They were added to the original portrait of the Virgin over the centuries. All these additions to the image — sunburst, crescent moon, etc. — were found to be deteriorating, while the original portrait showed no sign of wear, tear, or fading.

Another remarkable discovery related to the *tilma* was found, so to speak, in the eyes of the Virgin. Greatly enlarged photos of the eyes revealed a human figure resembling Juan Diego. Though this finding might be dismissed as an illusion, the *tilma* itself cannot be.

Like the Shroud of Turin, the reputed burial shroud of Jesus, the Guadalupe *tilma* is an object that the most rigorous examinations of modern science can't explain. This is its mystery for our own century. There are wonders in the rough cactus-fiber cloak that an Indian wore across his back on a December day many centuries ago. The Mother of God left her picture upon it as a sign of affection and protection for Juan's people and for all the Americas.

The apparitions of Our Lady of Guadalupe were never officially confirmed as "worthy of belief" in the same way that other apparitions were in later centuries. Perhaps the life-size image miraculously produced on the *tilma* of Juan Diego made that unnecessary. In 1754, however, Pope Benedict XIV authorized a Mass and Office under the title of Our Lady of Guadalupe for celebration on December 12, her feast day. Mary was also named patroness of New Spain (Mexico), and in 1910, Our Lady of Guadalupe was named patroness of Latin America. Pope Pius XII proclaimed the patronage of the Guadalupe Madonna over both continents (North and South America) in 1945.

CHAPTER 27

The Reality of Our Lady of Lourdes

By Rev. Jacob Restrick, O.P.

"Welcome, ladies and gentlemen, to Lourdes, France . . . please remain seated till the captain has turned off the seatbelt sign. . . ."

What exciting words to hear as I landed in September of 1988 on a chartered flight from New York with the National Rosary Pilgrimage — nearly three hundred sick and handicapped pilgrims accompanied by relatives, friends, priests, religious, and an energetic staff of doctors, nurses, and medics equipped to make our week's pilgrimage in Lourdes possible.

It was not my first visit to Lourdes, as I had come five years before. I was with one other brother, and we stayed at a quiet retreat house on the hillside facing the Grotto, far removed from the busy commercial streets leading to the Domain. This pilgrimage was quite different, as I was among several hundred others and would be staying in a small hotel typical of the four hundred two hotels in Lourdes: small, adequate, family-style meals at set hours, and in walking distance to the two gates (St. Joseph's and St. Michael's) that enter onto the Domain.

The crew at the Tarbes Airport is expert in disembarking passengers heading for Lourdes (a half-hour drive away). The airport is especially equipped for stretchers, wheelchairs, and nonambulatory passengers anxious to board their bus and get to their hotels. I wondered what thoughts and hopes were running through their heads as the adrenaline now felt gave us new energy after a long delay in taking off in New York and the nearly six-hour flight and time change that discombobulates a healthy seasoned traveler.

We're really here — in Lourdes — where Our Lady appeared to St. Bernadette in 1858; where millions of people have come ever since on pilgrimage. For what, I wondered? Did everyone come here hoping for a physical healing? Were some simply here to honor Our Lady in this Marian year, or to say "Thank you" for a blessing already received?

We were a "motley crowd" (I say with all love and respect). There were folks from California, Colorado, Texas, Illinois, Ohio, New Jersey, and New York — and those were just the ones I had met sitting near me on the plane. There were old and young, married couples, widowed, families, loners, and one engaged couple: our doctor and his fiancée from Florida. We were real Americans: black, white, Italian, Irish, Filipino, Korean, Japanese, Spanish, and combinations thereof. Some had come for many years on end; others several times before; but the majority were seeing Lourdes (and France) for the first time. The excitement we felt outdid any inconvenience we encountered in getting ourselves settled into the six hotels we would be occupying for the week.

The heart of Lourdes, of course, is the "Domain," that area surrounding the Grotto of the apparitions. The Domain is isolated from the rest of the town; within its thirty acres are the three basilicas built behind and above the cleft of rocks where Our Lady appeared. It is here that Bernadette dug in the earth, resulting in a spring of water gushing forth, which continues to flow to this day. There is an area to fill cups and bottles with the Lourdes water; there are also the "baths," where men and women enter in separate quarters to be immersed in pools of Lourdes water. There is an area for burning candles that, like the water, play a prominent part in the devotional life at Lourdes. These flank the Grotto, which is the heart of the Domain itself.

The underground basilica was completed in 1958 and named in honor of St. Pius X; it comfortably accommodates thousands and is easily accessible with wide cement ramps. There are also several hospices within the Domain that are like hospitals, in that they have wards set apart for pilgrims needing special medical care, and a nursing staff always present. Our ward was in the Hospice St. Bernadette with a huge window that overlooks the main basilica and the grotto.

In front of the basilica is a large esplanade for the outdoor processions. At the middle is a large crowned statue of Our Lady of Lourdes surrounded by a wrought-iron fence in which are placed small bouquets of flowers brought by departing pilgrims with the intention to return some day.

Our first scheduled event was the evening candlelight procession. We made our way through the narrow streets after supper, stopping to purchase a procession candle and paper "windcup" to prevent the candle from blowing out. We had an assigned starting position in the procession, marked by our American flag and a custom-made banner showing Our Lady and pilgrims under her mantle: Our Lady, Protectress of Pilgrims.

Over a public-address speaker the *Salve Regina* was intoned, and the pilgrims joined in singing this ancient Latin antiphon to Mary, "our life, our sweetness, and our hope." The Rosary then began with each Hail Mary in a different language, usually French, English, Italian, German, Dutch, and Spanish. One night I remember Japanese, Gaelic, and probably Vietnamese. The procession slowly begins to move. Candles are all lit. Latecomers are falling into step. And a holy stillness falls over the place that is awe-inspiring. The "Glory be" at the end of each decade is sung in Latin. Our group was always led by our several blind pilgrims, followed by a wheelchair "brigade" that always seemed to radiate a certain joy, followed by the others on foot, and in full voice.

Darkness came quickly and the glow of candles was even brighter than when we began. With the Rosary finished, the Lourdes hymn was sung, again in different languages on the verses, but on the refrain — "Ave, Ave, Ave Maria" — the whole throng sings in full voice, raising their torches over their heads in salute to the Mother of God. Hymns and prayers bring the procession to gather en masse before the Rosary Basilica. The bishops and priests present gather on the second level, flanked by the flags and banners from around the world. At the conclusion, a benediction is given with all the priests imparting their blessing to the thousands of pilgrims.

That was our first night, and this procession would be repeated each night of our pilgrimage. For me, this was one of the special moments to which I looked forward each night. To be in the midst of thousands of people singing and praying to the Blessed Virgin is an unforgettable experience of the Church.

After the evening procession the crowd would disperse: some to the hospice, some to their hotels, some to one of the many cafés that lined the streets. I made my way (as did many others) to the Grotto. The place of the apparitions is "busy" all day long; but late at night, when there's a chill in the air, there's a hushed silence that the darkness brings.

People gather in small groups or alone to pray, to kneel in the spot where Bernadette probably knelt, and to look at the familiar white alabaster statue that stands in the cleft of the rock. A line of pilgrims almost continuously files underneath in silence, touching and kissing the rock. It is never really noisy there, as if everyone senses the presence of Our Lady. It is here, I believe, at the heart of Lourdes that you find Our Lady, and she leads you to Jesus.

The Lord's presence in the Eucharist is very prominent at Lourdes. In the morning, our pilgrimage would meet each day at a different chapel, a different altar to celebrate Mass. The first day it was in the chapel of St. Joseph, the second morning it was at the Grotto itself, and near the end of the week it was at the outdoor altar of St. Bernadette, where our married couples renewed their marriage vows.

The highlight of the afternoon by far is the Eucharistic procession. Organized like the evening procession, it begins with the Rosary and singing of the Lourdes hymn. There are more wheelchairs and three-wheeled trolleys being pulled or pushed by friends, nurses, and men volunteers called brancardiers, who make it all run smoothly. If one is handicapped and alone at Lourdes, there is always someone to help.

This procession is especially for the sick who are given places of prominence on each side of the large area before the basilica. The Blessed Sacrament is carried solemnly under a canopy at the end of the procession. The priest carrying the monstrance makes his way slowly before the sick, stopping every few feet to bless them. Miracles and healings have been reported at this time. The procession ends with Benediction as thousands sing together the familiar *Tantum Ergo*.

The liturgical highlight of the week, however, is the Pilgrimage Mass for the Sick held each Wednesday in the underground basilica. Here the Church is gathered around the altar and in simple and dignified solemnity the whole People of God celebrate their union in Christ and proclaim the mystery of faith. The Liturgy of the Word is done in several languages; the chants are sung by a choir, but are easily singable by all. The concelebrants (over two hundred) flank the steps of the central high altar on all four sides; and the sick and handicapped are again given a prominent place close to the altar.

One fills up the day in any number of ways: There are life-size Stations of the Cross on the mountainside; there is a chapel with perpetual adoration as well as a chapel of reconciliation where confessionals, clearly marked by language groups, line the walls. There are the baths that are not limited to one visit per pilgrimage; many Lourdes travelers go every day. Even the most handicapped are welcomed and cared for by the brancardiers. There are places to visit, like Bernadette's home, a museum of memorabilia belonging to St. Bernadette. There is a movie as well as a slide show, and religious-goods stores are everywhere.

The time passed very quickly, and before we knew it, we were in our last candlelight procession the night before we left. We got to know each other well during the week. We were, as Pope Paul VI called the Church, a "Pilgrim People." The processions reminded me of that: everybody walking together, praying, poor, out of step, sick, and singing. The Church's sacramental life is alive at Lourdes with many tangible signs of God's loving care for His People. The water in which we are cleansed, healed, and refreshed — it is so much a part of Lourdes, and so much a reminder of our baptism. The flames of candle fire over our heads and descending upon us reminded me of Pentecost when the disciples were gathered around Mary, the Mother of the Lord, when the Spirit came upon them.

The priesthood is visible and reverenced both in the blessings at the end of the processions and in the confessionals and Masses being celebrated throughout the day in many languages. We had a liturgy that included the anointing of the sick, and another when vows of the sacrament of matrimony were renewed.

Yes, there were many little miracles among our pilgrims during the week: interior healings; healing of emotions; the return to grace; the acceptance of God's will in one's life; the strength to make decisions and commitments that would change one's life; the renewed awareness of the Holy Spirit's power in one's life; the renewed grace of Mary in all of our lives. No one, I believe, goes to Lourdes and returns the same person.

On my last night at the Grotto I noticed that many people seem to weep when they are there. I asked a Dominican Father who has been to Lourdes many times why he thought that was so. He said it was because it is as if the whole world has "come home to Mama." Coming home to Mama, to Mary our Mother. That was a wonderful way to put it.

CHAPTER 28
The Story of the Fátima Apparitions
By Catherine M. Odell

Of an evening during her early childhood, sometime in the autumn of 1916, Lucia dos Santos wrote, "It was the saddest supper I ever remember." Her mother, Maria Rosa, had wept with grief at the dinner table.

The family dos Santos, village peasants with seven children, had come upon some hard times in tiny Aljustrel, just half a mile south of Fátima, Portugal. Fátima itself was about seventy miles north of Lisbon, the capital. There was worry there and all over Portugal. The nation had entered World War I against Germany in March.

Manuel, one of Lucia's two brothers, was headed for military service. Then too, Antonio, the father and head of the family, had been turning to a life of drink and detachment from family duties. Without Manuel to help, Maria Rosa could see little to stop a steady downward slide of the family's precarious fortunes.

If Maria Rosa had been caught up in her own concerns during that year, so too had Lucia, the youngest of her seven children. The things that preoccupied mother and daughter, however, were almost literally worlds apart. Already that year, nine-year-old Lucia had witnessed the apparition of an angel three times. Maria Rosa knew nothing of it.

Early in the summer, Lucia, who tended the family's sheep, had been in a sort of cave near a place called Cabeco on land her father owned. She was with her cousins, eight-year-old Francisco Marto and his six-year-old sister, Jacinta. These two had persuaded their parents, Manuel (called Ti — "uncle" — by Lucia) and Olimpia Marto, that they too could tend the family flock, especially if Lucia was with them.

The sky had gone dark and a light rain had begun to fall. The three had run to the cave after they drove their sheep into the shelter of some trees. This area formed part of a mountain chain called the Serra da Estrela. It wriggles down the length of Portugal west past Fátima.

What came, however, was much more than a summer shower.

Suddenly, before the three shepherd children stood a shining young man of about fourteen or fifteen. He was, according to Lucia, incredibly handsome and "more brilliant than a crystal, penetrated by the rays of the sun." He calmed the children and told them he was the "Angel of Peace." Then the apparition asked the three to pray with him. Imitating his motions and his words, the cousins learned a prayer of adoration before the vision was gone, dissolving into the sun.

The children saw the Angel of Peace later in the summer and again in the autumn. From him they learned of the need for frequent prayer and sacrifice. The experiences had profoundly altered the lives of the three youngsters. Neither the Martos nor Lucia's parents suspected anything of this. Each day they sent out happy, playful children to herd and graze the sheep and goats. In private, however, the three children had begun a simple but deep prayer life and a habit of sacrifice and reparation that no one suspected.

All of this came to mind for Lucia the evening she saw her mother weeping at the table. The Angel of Peace had said, "Above all, accept and endure with submission the suffering which the Lord will send you." Lucia knew her mother was struggling to accept and endure. Lucia could not know that the following year would bring her own suffering — even from her mother, Maria Rosa. She did not know either that her heavenly Mother would bring her joy — face to face.

Sunday, May 13, 1917, was a fine, sunny day. Ti and Olimpia Marto thought so much of it that they took the cart to attend Mass at Batalha, a town to the west. After Mass, they told their children, they would head for the city's market to buy a piglet.

After they saw their parents off, Francisco and Jacinta,

now aged nine and seven, gathered the Marto sheep. They drove them to the place where they always met Lucia (now nearly ten) with the dos Santos flock. Together they moved the animals slowly to the Cova da Iria property that Antonio dos Santos owned. Once the animals were grazing, the three amused themselves while they kept an eye on the sheep.

They were busy creating a "house" out of a tangle of bushes and rocks. "Pretend" games were fun and always made the day go quickly. As they were lugging rocks to form a "wall" for the house, a flash of light against the clear blue sky startled them. Frightened by what they thought was lightning, the children ran down the slope toward a tree. Another flash cracked close to them there. They ran again — about a hundred yards — and found themselves staring at something atop a small evergreen tree called a *carrasqueira*, or holm oak.

It took three sets of normal, healthy eyes only a second to see that a large ball of light was settling at the top of the four-foot tree. Inside the glowing ball was the figure of a woman, a beautiful woman.

She was, as Lucia later wrote, "a Lady of all white, more brilliant than the sun dispensing light, clearer and more intense than a crystal cup full of crystalline water penetrated by the rays of the most glaring sun." Perhaps this description by Lucia as an adult would have overwhelmed her own childhood understanding. Her young cousins, who would never have the years of life to learn to write, put it more simply. There above the bush was a woman glowing with a bright light, they told others. The three of them were petrified.

"Don't be afraid," the woman said. "I won't hurt you." The tones were soothing, warm. Somehow, the voice melted their fear and drew them out of themselves into hope. They thought of the angel. This woman's presence was more peaceful, comforting.

"Where do you come from?" asked Lucia with great deference.

"I am from heaven," came the Lady's answer.

"And what is it you want of me?" Lucia asked after a moment.

The woman told her that she wanted the three to return on the thirteenth of each month at the same hour for six months in succession. They would see her at these times. At the end of the six months, she promised, she would tell them who she was and what she wanted. Lucia agreed that they would. Finding greater voice and courage, Lucia continued to quiz this mysterious woman.

"And shall I go to heaven too?" she inquired.

"Yes, you will."

"And Jacinta?"

"Also."

"And Francisco?"

"Also. But he will have to say more Rosaries!"

The Lady continued to answer Lucia's questions about hidden truths. Finally, the Lady asked Lucia if she and the other two would be willing to suffer all that would happen to them as a reparation for sins and for the conversion of sinners.

Without questioning her cousins, Lucia said "Yes." Then the woman told her that they would indeed suffer but that the grace of God would support them. At this, she spread her hands, and streams of light flowed from them toward the dusty red earth where the shepherd children stood.

Immediately, they felt an infusion of the light and of the presence of God. As though on cue, they dropped to their knees and began to utter prayers of divine adoration. The prayers came from somewhere deep inside. The woman watched over them until the prayer of praise came to a conclusion.

"Say the Rosary to obtain peace for the world and the end of the war," she told them.

Then, unlike the Angel of Peace who had dissolved into the light the year before, she rose from the bush and glided away into the eastern sky. Before their eyes, the woman became smaller and smaller until she was out of sight. The children studied the sky long after she was gone.

Then it was as though they themselves had to return to earth.

"Oh, such a pretty Lady!" Jacinta finally said.

In a moment, all three were talking excitedly of what they'd seen and what it meant. Lucia and Jacinta told Francisco all that the Lady said. Although he had seen her, he could not hear her, just as he had not heard the angel the year before.

The children drove the sheep back to Aljustrel early. On the way, Lucia warned her cousins to keep silent about the Lady from heaven. But looking at Jacinta made her wonder if the secret could be kept. The seven-year-old's face was absolutely radiant. Was the joy too large for Jacinta to hold inside? On the following morning, Lucia would find out.

The youngest of the dos Santos children went to bed as usual, having given no hint of what the day had brought. In the morning, she ate and went out to play alone. In a way, she was a lonely child in this family. Her oldest sisters, Maria of the Angels and Theresa, had already been married when Lucia was born. Caroline, the sister next to her in age, was fifteen — too old to play little-girl games. In the midst of her daydreaming, Lucia heard the voice of Maria of the Angels.

"Oh, Lucia! I hear you have seen Our Lady at Cova da Iria!"

Lucia looked up at her grinning sister but gave no answer. Jacinta or Francisco had told. She knew that there would be trouble. She bit her lip and wondered what others would have to say. The tale would be taken from house to house before sundown.

Within half an hour, Lucia was called into the house. Her mother and father wanted to know what had happened the day before. Very simply, she told them of the flash of light, the appearance of the Lady dressed in white, and the Lady's claim to be from heaven. She left out nothing but was troubled by what she saw upon the faces of her parents.

In fact, Antonio, her father, dismissed the matter. "Silly women's tales!" he muttered. He got up and left without giving Lucia a second glance. Maria Rosa was furious. She had taught her children to tell the truth, and she shouted at her nearly ten-year-old daughter. Now her youngest would make her old age miserable by becoming a liar. Lucia could protest no further. She left the house when her mother dismissed her and, with tears streaming down her face, headed for the sheep pen.

On the road, Lucia walked slowly, tapping her sheep on the rump with a stick to keep them moving. Then she spotted Francisco and Jacinta. Even from the distance, she could see their misery. She said nothing as she neared the wide spot in the road where they were waiting for her.

Francisco was fighting back tears. Jacinta was weeping with her face in her hands. They had evidently heard of the trouble they had caused at the dos Santos house. "Don't cry any more," said Lucia, going then to her cousins with her arms outstretched for them. Her own anger vanished.

As they watched the flock that day, the day after the first apparition, the children were sad. The secret joy of the experience seemed lost. Wearing a long face, Jacinta sat on a rock. Finally, the three began to talk. Jacinta said she wanted to pray the full Rosary and do sacrifices as the Lady had asked. The children had always prayed a daily Rosary, but they had taken shortcuts, merely saying the words "Our Father" and "Hail Mary" instead of the complete prayers. And after a discussion, the cousins settled on a sacrifice. They would give their lunches to the sheep.

As May passed, Lucia endured a continual barrage of sarcastic or threatening attacks at home. The opposition of her mother was most painful. Maria Rosa was offended by the gossip and snickering of her neighbors. At the Marto house-hold, Olimpia was indifferent. But Ti Marto believed in his children. He knew they were not liars.

"If you don't say it was a lie, I will lock you up in a dark room where you will never see the light of the sun again," Maria Rosa fumed at Lucia. But Lucia would not deny a word of it. She suffered an agony of spirit and looked toward the thirteenth of June.

As the date of the next apparition came closer, Lucia's mother and sisters began to tempt her with reminders about the festival that day. June 13 was also the feast of St. Anthony of Padua, one of the greatest feasts in Portugal. Lucia remembered very well that there would be a great procession, with flowers, dancing, fireworks, and a delicious bread given to all the children. It was a day she loved, but she knew she would be at the Cova.

Well before dawn on the thirteenth, Lucia had her flock out to pasture in order to return them early. She attended Mass at Fátima to honor St. Anthony. When she returned home, she found a group of neighbors who wanted to accompany her to the Cova. She did not like the idea, but Maria Rosa liked it even less. The sight of such "gullible" adults and children was enraging. A flurry of sarcastic, biting comments from her mother and sisters poured down upon Lucia.

"I felt very, very bitter that day," Lucia wrote years later. "I recalled the times that were past, and I asked myself where was the affection that my family had had for me only a little while ago."

The small crowd and the three children left for the Cova at 11:00 A.M. Lucia was crying softly, but Francisco cheered her up. Just before the appointed hour, noon, they sat on the ground near the *carrasqueira* and waited. They recited the Rosary, and those who had escorted the children opened picnic baskets to eat. One girl led the Litany of Our Lady until Lucia stood up and interrupted her.

"Jacinta," she said, "there comes Our Lady! There is the light!"

Everyone stood up. Bystanders noticed that the sun seemed to dim even in the cloudless sky. Others noticed that the small *carrasqueira* bent a little at the top. The Lady had appeared again.

Again, Lucia asked the vision what she wanted of her. Again, the Lady requested that the children come the next month and that they recite five decades of the Rosary each day. She also told the girl that she wanted the children to learn to read, and that further instructions would follow later. Lucia then asked the Lady if she would take the three of them to heaven.

This time, the answer was more specific. The Lady promised to take Francisco and Jacinta to heaven with her soon. But for Lucia, there was a different plan. She was to remain on earth longer to help establish worldwide devotion to the Lady's Immaculate Heart.

"I stay here alone?" Lucia asked with sadness.

The woman answered her with great tenderness. She would never really be alone, Lucia was told. "My Immaculate Heart will be your refuge." With that, the woman extended her hands. Great showers of light seemed to pour forth as before, but one shaft seemed to flow down upon Lucia. The other radiated back up to the sky from the sister and brother. All three saw a vision of the Immaculate Heart. As in May, the children were flooded with an unearthly joy and peace. Then the woman rose again and traveled into the eastern sky.

When the children were finally left alone, Lucia, Jacinta, and Francisco walked back together to Aljustrel. The girls told Francisco what the Lady had said. He was delighted once again to hear that his trip to heaven was assured. When the three split up to go home, the Marto children again earned a skeptical but neutral reception. Lucia, on the other hand, encountered a household that was, if anything, more abrasive than before as she told of the encounter. The following day, Maria Rosa dragged the girl to the pastor to see if he could make her recant the story.

Father Ferreira was gentle with the girl, but he told the mother and daughter that Lucia might be experiencing visions from a diabolical source. Lucia was frightened and depressed. Jacinta and Francisco were convinced that the Lady showed no traits of the evil one. "And we saw her go up to heaven," Jacinta reasoned.

Lucia had no one to help her sort it out. Maria Rosa's brutal antagonism never let up. During this month the fear grew that the devil was disguising himself as a beautiful lady from heaven. "Would the devil take her away?" she asked herself. Lucia decided not to go to the Cova for the apparitions any more.

Almost at the last moment on July 13, Lucia ran to the Martos' cottage and found Francisco and Jacinta in tears. They weren't going either, they explained. "We don't dare go without you," they told her. Lucia was the spokesman, the leader, and her cousins knew it.

Instantly, the girl's heart was changed. "I've changed my mind, and I'm going," she told them. Francisco told Lucia that they had been praying for her all night long. In thirty seconds, they were out of the house and off to their rendezvous with the Lady. Nearly three thousand people awaited the children at the Cova. Among them were two mothers who had come with blessed candles to banish the devil. Ti Marto had also come to protect his children from the crowds.

At noon, the woman came again. Much of the apparition unfolded like the others. Lucia again asked what the Lady wanted. Again she passed on the requests for healings. Again the Lady asked the children's return on the appointed days and requested the Rosary each day for peace. She did refer to herself as "Our Lady of the Rosary." Then something totally new took place.

The Lady spread her hands as before, but this time the light poured through the children into the earth below them. The inner regions of the earth seemed to open and the three children looked into hell. "A sea of fire; and plunged in this fire the demons and the souls, as if they were red-hot coals," Lucia wrote of it years later. The crowd could see that the children were oppressed by some horror.

The Lady acknowledged that they had looked into hell but explained that many souls could be saved from damnation by devotion to her Immaculate Heart and by reparation. Prophecies continued: If offenses against God did not stop, the Lady told them, another more terrible war would begin in the reign of Pope Pius XI. If this meant little to the three peasant children, the warning astounded others, who knew that Pope Benedict XV was then the reigning Pontiff.

The Lady also had other requests to make, global requests. "I come to ask the consecration of Russia to my Immaculate Heart and the Communion of reparation on the first Saturdays," she said. "If they listen to my requests, Russia will be converted and there will be peace. If not, she will scatter her errors through the world, provoking wars and persecution of the Church." Some of these persecutions would touch the Holy Father, the Pope, she continued.

"In the end my Immaculate Heart will triumph," she said finally. "The Holy Father will consecrate Russia to me, and it will be converted and a certain period of peace will be granted to the world. In Portugal the dogma of the faith will always be kept."

Then there were private things to say to the children. The Lady of the Immaculate Heart told Lucia and Jacinta to share all of these messages with Francisco. Then she gave the children a final secret not to be told to anyone.

When the Lady rose into the east this time, the children were pale. They stared at one another but could think of no words to describe what they had seen or heard. Somehow, the crowd knew that this appearance was different from the others. As they mobbed the children, throwing questions at them, Ti Marto scooped up his youngest, Jacinta, and started to lead the children away. All three seemed to carry away the weight of profound promises and threats on which the world would turn. Something of their childhood was left behind.

After the July apparition, all of Portugal knew of Fátima. Steady streams of visitors descended upon Aljustrel. There was no privacy now for the Martos or for the dos Santos family. "It's too bad you didn't keep quiet," a frustrated Francisco complained one day to Jacinta. When they saw visitors heading down the road toward their homes, they would hide.

In Lucia's household, however, there was renewed anger

over the matter. Her father discovered that the crowds had trampled and destroyed his vegetable gardens at the Cova. A hungry winter was more likely for Lucia's family. They would not let her forget it. Only in the hills with the sheep was there any peace. But the negative attitude went far beyond Lucia's house.

In 1910, a Portuguese republic had come to power after the assassination of King Carlos. The republic was openly anticlerical and hostile to religion. The Fátima-generated upsurge of piety had to be stopped for political reasons, many Portuguese officials reasoned.

With this thought in mind, the administrator of Ourem arrived in Aljustrel on August 13, 1917. He claimed to have had a religious conversion. He would personally take the three children to the apparition, he promised. The Martos were reluctant. Antonio dos Santos did not care how his daughter got there. Finally, however, the visionaries were driven off in a wagon to the Cova by the newest "believer."

Halfway there, the administrator turned around and took them back to his house at Ourem. They missed the apparition and were grieved about it. For two days, the children were locked away and threatened with death unless they revealed "the secret" Our Lady had given them. On the second day of captivity, they were taken out of a jail cell one by one. The administrator told them that they would be boiled in oil. Jacinta was carried away first and sequestered to frighten the others. "What do we care if they kill us?" Francisco whispered to a pale Lucia. "We go straight to heaven!"

At that, the agnostic administrator of Ourem knew that he was defeated. On August 15, he took the children back to Aljustrel and left them on the steps of the rectory. On Sunday, August 19, the Virgin came to the children during the afternoon in a hollow, or low valley, called Valinhos.

After she was gone, the children cut branches from the *carrasqueria* on which she had settled and took them home. The scent of the branches was particularly sweet to Maria Rosa, but she still did not believe in the Lady or in Lucia's claims.

Early on the thirteenth of September, the three young visionaries struggled through a crowd of thousands to get to the Cova. This apparition was very short. The Lady promised that at the next appearance the children would also see the Lord, Our Lady of Sorrows, Our Lady of Mount Carmel, and St. Joseph with the Child Jesus. "Continue to say the Rosary to bring about the end of the war," she reminded them. Then after promising the cure of some who had asked for healing, she disappeared into the east.

The time between this and the last appearance on October 13 passed quickly for Aljustrel and for the three young visionaries. As the thirteenth dawned rainy and windy, more than seventy thousand people were camped at the Cova waiting for noon and for a break in the rain. With anxiety, the parents of the children prepared to go. They feared that if there was no miracle the children would be killed by an angry crowd.

Just before noon, Lucia and her cousins waited for the Virgin. Though she could not explain why, she told the crowd to close their umbrellas. The rain continued to come but changed into a lighter mist. Looking into the east, Lucia was suddenly transformed.

"Watch out, daughter, don't let yourself be deceived," cautioned her doubtful mother.

The three children did not hear this last expression of disbelief that Maria Rosa would make. On their knees they gazed up at the Lady who had come again to rest on the little *carrasqueira* decorated with flowers and garlands. A fine mist sprayed their faces.

"What do you want of me?" Lucia began again for the last time.

"I want to tell you to have them build a chapel here in my honor. I am the Lady of the Rosary. Let them continue to say the Rosary every day. The war is going to end, and the soldiers will soon return to their homes."

The child asked again for the cures of many of the sick.

The Lady of the Rosary promised the healing of some, but added that they must amend their lives and ask pardon for their sins. "Let them offend Our Lord God no more, for He is already much offended," she added.

These were the last words the Lady would speak to Lucia and to the world at Fátima. She opened her hands again, and the light that came from them shot skyward. "Look at the sun!" Lucia shouted. The promised miracle was beginning, but the Virgin Mother of God vanished.

The crowds looked up to see clouds roll back and reveal the sun. But it was now like a disk of white light that all could look at without blinking. Meanwhile, all three children viewed a tableau in the heavens of scenes representing the mysteries of the Rosary. At the Joyful Mysteries, they saw the Holy Family and watched St. Joseph bless the crowds three times. The Christ Child was in his arms. Lucia then saw visions of Our Lady of Sorrows, and then of Our Lady of Mount Carmel.

At the same time, the crowds watched in awe as the sun bobbed in the sky like a bright silver top. Then the "dancing sun" stopped and began to spin. As it whirled, bright rays representing every color of the spectrum shot off and washed everything on the earth. Green, red, violet worlds appeared momentarily to surround the people, who shouted and praised God.

Then seventy thousand there at the Cova watched the sun plunge in a zigzag path toward the earth. In every heart there was a fear of death. People fell to their knees by the hundreds. Just as the sun seemed about to strike the earth, it stopped and was suddenly returned to its proper place and its proper brightness. The crowd noticed that all clothing, previously soaked with rain, had dried. The "Miracle of the Sun" was seen in nearby cities. There was no serious talk of mass hallucination. Portugal was convinced.

Lucia, Jacinta, and Francisco were mobbed and then hoisted onto the shoulders of some sturdier men. After hours of trying to break free of the questioners, they were returned home pale and exhausted. In the following months, the mothers of Lucia and Jacinta agreed to send the girls to school so they could learn to read. The Lady had requested that. Francisco declined the opportunity, knowing that he would leave the world before reading could be useful. He spent much of his time praying in the Church of St. Anthony at Fátima.

On April 4, 1919, Francisco died of bronchial pneumonia. He was not quite eleven years old. "What a man he would have been," said his father sadly. Long before the apparitions, he had been very proud of this youngest son, a handsome boy who loved nature and never showed fear. Lucia visited him every day during his long illness. Seeing that he was close to death, she asked him to pray for her from heaven.

Jacinta was already sick as well. She was devastated by the loss of her brother's presence but rejoiced in his better fortune. Over the summer and fall she developed pleurisy, which became increasingly serious. On February 20, 1920, in a Lisbon hospital, she died at 10:30 P.M. As she had predicted, there was no one with her when Our Lady of the Rosary came to welcome her.

Left alone to bear the burden of witness, Lucia remained for several years with her family. At fourteen, in June of 1921, she left Aljustrel in the middle of the night for a school run by the Sisters of St. Dorothy at Porto.

In 1925, Lucia decided to enter the convent of the Sisters of St. Dorothy. Still, none in her convent knew of her real identity as the surviving child of Fátima. In 1930, the bishop recognized the apparitions at Fátima, declaring that they were indeed "worthy of belief." Cures by the hundreds were being reported there, although a massive wave of anti-Catholic fervor was otherwise threatening the nation.

In 1936, Sister Maria das Dores (Mary of Sorrows) penned the first account of the apparitions in obedience to a request by the bishop. Three other accounts were produced, one in 1937 and two in 1941.

On May 13, 1982, Pope John Paul II traveled to Fátima, where he met the only living witness of the apparitions. This

Pope believed he owed his survival after an assassination attempt to the Immaculate Heart of Mary. He had been shot exactly one year before. Then he consecrated the world to the Immaculate Heart in collegial union with the bishops of the Church.

Today, millions visit the shrine at Fátima in Portugal. Millions more have been transformed by the message brought by Our Lady to three children in the most important series of apparitions in modern times.

CHAPTER 29
Ecumenical Impact
of Marian Apparitions

By Rev. Paul D. Lee

(Editor's note: The following was delivered to the Ecumenical Society of the Blessed Virgin Mary at their Spring 1999 meeting in Washington, D.C.)

Apparition stories of Mary seem to have the most perdurable and widespread following. Although not limited to this century, the sheer number of claimed Marian apparitions in the twentieth century is quite astounding. Beginning with Tung Lu, China, in 1900, up to Brooklyn, U. S. A., in 1996, there are 386 cases of Marian apparitions. The Church has made "no decision" about the supernatural character to 299 of the 386 cases; "negative decisions" from the Church about the supernatural character are 79 out of 386.

The Church has said "yes" in terms of the supernatural character of only eight cases: Fátima (Portugal), Beauraing (Belgium), Banneux (Belgium), Akita (Japan), Syracuse (Italy), Zeitoun (Egypt), Manila (Philippines) (according to some sources), and Betania (Venezuela). The information is available from the University of Dayton website.

Local bishops have approved of the faith expression at the sites where these eight apparitions occurred. Besides the eight approved apparitions, there have been eleven (out of the 386 apparitions) that have not been approved with a "supernatural character" but have received a "yes" to indicate the local bishop's "approval of faith expression (prayer and devotion) at the site." Every day, there are thousands of people visiting these places as pilgrimage sites to pray and to experience the divine presence.

If these apparitions are a "Catholic thing" — borrowing the expression from Rosemary Haughton, *The Catholic Thing*

(Springfield, Illinois: Templegate Publishers, 1979) — then why is it an ecumenical matter? Is there an ecumenical impact of Marian apparitions? First, most concern Mary, who has been an eminently suitable topic for Church unity as diverse members and traditions in the Church struggle to find one voice on the topic. Second, if Christians are to recover unity as one Body of Christ, they cannot ignore Mary or turn their eyes from these apparitions. Third, there are theological, spiritual, and pastoral matters and problems regarding those apparitions that are not limited to the Catholic Church, as will be evident later. Fourth, as we begin the new millennium, our focus is on celebrating the year of Jubilee in acknowledging the two thousandth year of the Incarnation of the Son of God. At this juncture we need to examine if we are effective ambassadors of Christ to one another and to the world. John 17:21 is a perennial reminder of our noble mission toward unity and evangelization. As the disciple of Jesus par excellence, Mary remains the foremost model of faith and unity with the Lord in thought, word, and deed. In particular, the milleniarist anxiety, misled by absurd apocalyptic messages of warnings, punishment, and impending doom, is often associated with the apparitions. A theological and spiritual examination of this issue is a necessity across the denominational boundaries.

We will more closely observe these private revelations in terms of the criteria and norms for discerning their authenticity. The inherent and implicit theological issues will be considered, and finally, we will attempt to assess the impacts of apparitions to the efforts toward Christian unity.

In order to contextualize these issues for better understanding, however, we need to examine briefly the prevailing and customary areas of concern regarding Mary in ecumenical dialogue.

The topics of the Blessed Virgin Mary are wide-ranging and controversial, thus easily divisive. Even if she is not the cause of division among churches, she has become the sign of separation. It is understandable, because underlying the issue of Mary are soteriology, anthropology, ecclesiology, the inter-pretation of Scripture, the development of doctrine, and Tradi-tion.

Traditional points of discussion and controversy are: (1) Mary's cooperation with the saving work of Christ; (2) the two Marian dogmas defined in 1854 and 1950, the Immaculate Conception and the Assumption; (3) the perpetual virginity of the Virgin Mary; and (4) the invocation of Mary in liturgical and popular devotion.

Marian Topics in Ecumenical Dialogues

These are recurring themes in most of the bilateral dia-logues as well (see Giancarlo Bruni, "Mariologia ecumenica? Indicazioni dal dialogo ecumenico," *Marianum* (1997), LIX 152, pp. 601-650).

Classical Pentecostals see the point of divergence in terms of doctrinal development as well as doctrinal differences, es-pecially in the area of Mary's relationship to the Church and Mary's role in the communion of saints. Clarifications have been made on the motherhood, veneration, intercession, vir-ginity of Mary, Catholic doctrine on the graces given to Mary, and the two major Marian dogmas. The constant Pentecostal concern is the scriptural basis of the doctrines and practices (see "Final Report of the Dialogue between the Secretariat for Promoting Christian Unity of the Roman Catholic Church and Some Classical Pentecostals [1977-1982]," in *Deepening Com-munion: International Ecumenical Documents with Roman Catholic Participants*, edited by William Rusch and J. Gros [Washington, D.C./Mahwah, New Jersey: United States Catho-lic Conference/Paulist Press, 1998], pp. 379-397).

Evangelicals express their uneasiness, fear, or objection regarding some of the expressions in reference to Mary, used by Catholics, such as "the Associate of the Redeemer," "coop-eration," "mediatrix," and "immersed in the mystery of the Trin-ity." As Evangelicals reveal their apprehension toward the Catholic emphasis in Mary's role in salvation and some ambiguous and misleading vocabulary, Catholics are "troubled by . . . a notable neglect by Evangelicals of the place given by God to Mary in salvation history and in the life of the Church" ("The Evangelical-Roman Catholic Dialogue on Mission [1977-1984]," in *Deepening Communion,* p. 454).

The main area of difficulty in the Anglican-Roman Catholic conversation on Marian doctrine concerns not only the content of the doctrine but also the exercise of teaching authority, (see "The Final Report, Authority in the Church I," 24, [c] and "Authority in the Church II," 30, in *Called to Full Unity: Documents on Anglican-Roman Catholic Relations 1966-1983* [Washington, D.C.: United States Catholic Conference, 1986], pp. 263, 280-281).

A more focused and thorough treatment of the Marian issues is found in the Lutheran-Catholic dialogue dealing with "The One Mediator, the Saints, and Mary." While Lutherans speak of God for us (*pro nobis*) in Christ and of unmerited salvation outside us (*extra nos*), the sole mediatorship of Christ over against the invocation of the saints and Mary is maintained because of the uniqueness of Christ's work. Christ is not only the sole Mediator, but also the One Who is mediated (see *The One Mediator, the Saints, and Mary: Lutherans and Catholics in Dialogue VIII,* edited by H. G. Anderson, J. Francis Stafford, and J. A. Burgess [Minneapolis: Augsburg, 1992], p. 44). For Catholics too, this unique mediatorship is reserved for Christ, yet the term is applied to exemplary believers in a derivative sense, which is creaturely cooperation: "So also the sole mediation of the Redeemer does not exclude but rather gives rise to a cooperation that varies on the part of creatures and that is but a sharing (*participitatem*) from this one source (*ex unico fonte*)" (*Lumen Gentium,* No. 61).

Baptists also show their concern over the sole mediatorship of Jesus and the lack of explicit scriptural grounding of the Marian dogmas. Catholics are urged to understand these concerns, while Baptists are invited to understand the biblical and theological backgrounds of Marian doctrine and devotion as well as its significance in popular piety and religious practice (see "Summons to Witness to Christ in Today's World [July 23, 1988]," Nos. 56-57 in *Deepening Communion,* p. 358).

The unofficial but highly regarded *Groupe des Dombes* has recently studied Marian issues under two principles (salient points are summarized in "Ecumenical Document on Mary," in *The Marian Library Newsletter* No. 37, New Series, Winter, 1998-1999):

1. The doctrine of the justification of faith in Christ Jesus is the defining article of the Reformed churches, affirmed by the Catholic Church at Trent and most recently in the international Lutheran-Catholic dialogue (see Lutheran World Federation and the Pontifical Council for Promoting Christian Unity, *Joint Declaration on the Doctrine of Justification* (June 25, 1998), in *Origins* 28:8, July 16, 1998).

2. Vatican II's principle of the "hierarchy of truths" (*Unitatis Redintegratio*, No.11), in which certain truths are fundamental and central (for example, the Trinity, the Incarnation, the Redemption) and other truths are dependent on the foundation of the Christian faith. Catholics do not believe that those who do not hold these truths are, on that account, excluded from heaven.

The balance and caliber of *Groupe des Dombes* is instructive and refreshing. In most dialogues a heavy focus is on the soteriological question with regard to Mary and the relationship between Scripture and Tradition, thus the feasibility of the doctrinal development. The relative lack of attention to the significance of devotion and practice on the popular level is understandable; still it is a lack. Moreover, there is a total silence about Marian apparitions in the dialogues, which have been a significant, if not essential, part of Marian devotion. Thus, these two topics need to be examined.

Significance of Popular Marian Piety

The Blessed Virgin Mary has occupied an extraordinary place in popular Christianity and even in evangelization. The most powerful religious symbol for young American Catholics is the crèche. The most popular Catholic symbol is the Rosary. We are told:

> The development of popular religion has always contained a threat to the heart of the Christian Faith, namely to the belief that salvation is only through Jesus Christ, the Word of God made flesh, and that sinners are justified by grace alone through faith alone. . . . Yet there are pastoral opportunities in popular piety . . . to bring consolation and hope to the poor in terms that used the senses of sight and hearing to reach the mind and heart. It freed the imagination of the simple folk in relation to the divine.
>
> — George Tavard, "The Veneration of Saints as Ecumenical Question," in *Walking Together: Roman Catholics and Ecumenism Twenty-Five Years after Vatican II*, edited by Thaddeus D. Horgan (Grand Rapids, Michigan: Eerdmans, 1990, p. 129)

The profound faith of these simple folk has nurtured innumerable people in their lifelong journey to God. It is not necessarily the sophistication of theology, or the accuracy of doctrine, or just the Scriptures that contribute to the growth of faith, leading to the saving encounter and relationship with God. Theologically speaking, God cannot be constrained to using a limited list of means of communication. Importance of popular piety is emphatically affirmed in the 1997 Synod of American Bishops:

> A distinctive feature of America is an intense popular piety, deeply rooted in the various nations. It is found at all levels and in all sectors of society, and it has special importance as a place of encounter with Christ for all those who in poverty of spirit and humility of heart are sincerely searching for God (see Mt 11:25). This piety takes many forms: "Pilgrimages to shrines of Christ, of

191

the Blessed Virgin and the Saints, prayer for the souls in purgatory, the use of sacramentals (water, oil, candles . . .). These and other forms of popular piety are *an opportunity for the faithful to encounter the living Christ.*" The Synod Fathers stressed *the urgency of discovering the true spiritual values present in popular religiosity,* so that, enriched by genuine Catholic doctrine, it might lead to a sincere conversion and a practical exercise of charity. If properly guided, popular piety also leads the faithful to a deeper sense of their membership in the Church, increasing the fervor of their attachment and thus offering an effective response to the challenges of today's secularization.

> — John Paul II, *The Church in America (Ecclesia in America): On the Encounter with the Living Jesus Christ: The Way to Conversion, Communion, and Solidarity in America,* Post-Synodal Apostolic Exhortation (Washington, D.C.: United States Catholic Conference, 1999, pp. 29-30)

In fact, evangelization is more than the proclamation of the Word, but eventually we Christians intend to "bring the Good News into all areas of humanity, and through its impact, to transform that humanity from within, making new"(Paul VI, *Evangelii Nuntiandi*). Therefore evangelization, which includes popular piety, also searches out the proper way of enculturation. Given that in America, popular piety is a mode of enculturation of the Catholic faith and that it has often assumed indigenous religious forms, we must not underestimate the fact that, prudently considered, it too can provide valid cues for a more complete enculturation of the Gospel. This is especially important among the indigenous peoples, in order that "the seeds of the Word" found in their culture may come to their fullness in Christ. The same is true for Americans of African origin. The Church "recognizes that it must approach these Americans from within their own culture, taking seriously the spiritual and human riches of that culture which appear in the way they worship, their sense of joy and solidarity, their language and their traditions" (*Ecclesia in America*, p. 16).

While the objective hierarchy of truths serves well for ecumenical progress charting the map for the journey, we may consider the *existential* hierarchy of truths as proposed by Karl Rahner. A poor peasant in a remote village may be deprived of proper catechesis, yet his faithful devotion to Mary will serve well in maintaining his relationship with God. The objective hierarchy of truths may be somewhat off, but its intended purpose would be fulfilled.

Groupe des Dombes indicates a threefold role that Mary plays in popular Christianity: (1) *Closeness, Proximity* — she is the mother attentive to her children. (2) *Cultural Identity* — she has been integrated into and celebrated as part of the culture. (3) *Protector and Healer* — she liberates from oppression and is a source of healing.

Already the Council of Nicaea II, held in 787, distinguished "full adoration" (*latria*) directed to God alone, and "respectful veneration" (*dulia*) to the saints (see *Decrees of the Ecumenical Councils*, Vol. 1, edited by N. Tanner [London/ Washington, D.C: Sheed and Ward/Georgetown University Press, 1990], p. 136). Marian devotion "fits into the only worship that is rightly called Christian, because it takes its origin and effectiveness from Christ, finds its complete expression in Christ, and leads through Christ in the Spirit to the Father"(Paul VI, *Marialis Cultus*, 1974, Introduction). Among Marian devotees, this orientation is quite clear.

Silence About Mary?

Marian piety cannot and should not be a unique Catholic property. The authentic Marian piety should characterize the life of every Christian, because Mary occupies an active presence through the Church's history. At its beginning (the mystery of the Incarnation), in its being set up (the mystery of Cana and of the Cross), and in its manifestation (the mystery of Pentecost), she is present at the center of the pilgrim Church (see Congregation for Catholic Education, *The Virgin Mary in Intellectual and Spiritual Formation*, Rome, March 25, 1988, Nos. 33, 17).

Groupe des Dombes explains that the silence of the Reformed churches on Mary originates not from the sixteenth century but from the post-Reformation polemics. The Virgin Mary became the sign of Catholic orthodoxy: She was invoked as protectress of the Church against its enemies, as the "Conqueror of Heresy." Only in the twentieth century have some Protestant churches experienced an awakening of interest in Mary, derived from studies of the early Church, the rediscovery of the Reformers, and the influence of the liturgical movement. In addition, the Second Vatican Council's consideration of Mary is definitely Christocentric, biblical, liturgical, ecumenical, and anthropological.

Hence, *Groupe* challenges Protestants to examine whether their silence regarding the Virgin Mary is consistent with the thinking of the original Reformers, and whether this silence has enhanced or diminished their representation of Christ and His saving work:

> Karl Barth, who was so critical of some aspects of Catholic positions toward Mary, would not have the Virgin Mary relegated to obscurity. "In her, there is someone greater than Abraham, than Moses, than David, than John the Baptist, than Paul, and the whole Christian Church. Here we have the Mother of the Lord, the Mother of Him Who is God. She is an altogether unique creature."
>
> — *Groupe des Dombes*, "Ecumenical Document on Mary," in *The Marian Library Newsletter* No. 37, New Series, Winter, 1998-1999

In ecumenical dialogue statements, there are some references to Marian popular piety, but there is a complete silence about Marian apparitions. What does that signify?

Silence About Marian Apparitions

Without denying the elements of sensationalism and commercialism, while acknowledging the danger of false claims and misguided reports, many of these apparitions have achieved noble Gospel purposes: personal and ecclesial conversion, habit of prayer, regular reception of the sacraments, humility, practice of fasting and almsgiving, and so on. (George Tavard says, "Visions multiply by imitation," meaning that a well-known apparition seems to encourage reports of similar ones. This is literally true in the electronic communication. It is simply an eye-opener to witness the astounding variety of "Apparition websites.")

This is particularly true in some of the well-known apparitions, such as Guadalupe (1531), Paris (1830), Lourdes (1858), Knock (1879), Fátima (1917), and Banneux (1933). In many cases, Mary appeared to humble people and simple children. Unlike so many apocalyptic messages of doom among claimed apparitions, the primary message to these favored individuals is about returning to the practice of the fundamental and simple Gospel call, as just mentioned. The silence about the apparitions in ecumenical dialogues is due to lack of experience on the part of the non-Catholic dialogue partners. This has become a characteristically Catholic happening. Experience shows, however, that places such as Lourdes provide an opportunity for spiritual renewal and conversion not exclusively for Catholics.

The Catholic Church's Discernment

The Catholic Church takes very deliberate steps of discernment (see The Sacred Congregation for the Doctrine of the Faith, *Norms of the Congregation for Proceeding in Judging Alleged Apparitions and Revelations,* Vatican, February 25, 1978). It is the responsibility of the local bishop to conduct an investigation, usually through a committee of experts. Norms for discernment are:

1. There should be moral certainty, or at least great prob-

ability, that something miraculous has occurred; thus, there must be no doubt that what is occurring is truly exceptional and beyond human explanation.

2. The subjects who claim to have had the apparition must be mentally sound, honest, sincere, of upright conduct, obedient to ecclesiastical authorities, and able to return to the normal practices of the faith. There must be no hint of financial advantage to anyone connected with the apparitions.

3. The content of the revelation or message must be theologically acceptable, morally sound, and free of error. There must be no doctrinal error attributed to God or to the Blessed Virgin Mary or some other saint.

4. The apparition must result in positive spiritual assets that endure (prayer, conversion, increase of charity).

At the end of the investigative process, the committee may submit to the bishop (or bishops, as the case may be) one of the following verdicts or conjectural judgments: (1) *constat de supernaturalitate* (the event shows all the signs of being an authentic or a truly miraculous intervention from heaven); (2) *constat de non supernaturalitate* (the alleged apparition is clearly not miraculous or there are not sufficient signs manifesting it to be so); (3) *non constat de supernaturalitate* (it is not evident whether or not the alleged apparition is authentic). The bishop's decision regarding alleged apparitions usually does not attempt to interpret or give the spiritual significance of the events, nor to interpret the messages or identify the heavenly persons who may have appeared.

Spiritual and Theological
Understanding of Apparitions

Why are there so many apparitions? Perhaps the phenomena reflect the genuine spiritual hunger and thirst of people. It is true, however, that God's desire for us is incomparably greater than our desire for God. Genuine apparitions always stem from the divine initiative, over which humans have no control. In simplistic terms, God is eagerly searching, and people are responding. Staggering numbers of books on apparitions apparently correspond to the broad readership. A spiritual caveat to these "seekers" is that constantly seeking one "mountaintop experience" after another is a sure way of spiritual failure. Genuine Marian piety is always related to Christ and His paschal mystery; miracles and apparitions are only indicators of the reality.

Some Christians talk about direct and immediate communication and access to God without other mediation. There is no pure experience of the Divine. There is no immediacy to the divine presence for the earthly pilgrims. Every experience is through mediation. Every account of the encounter with God is an interpretation. Mediation, especially in a sacramental way, is the mode of Christian existence. Sacramentality of faith is the mode of perception of faith for the pilgrims on earth. The encounter is real, but in the sacramental realm. The experiences are filtered through our relating to the sensory and epistemological purview.

In this sense, Divine Revelation can be understood as "symbolic communication." Avery Dulles, an advocate of this term, mentions four qualities of symbol and revelation to show the advantage of this concept: (1) Symbolism gives participatory knowledge; revelation also gives participatory awareness, involving one in the life of the faith community to share the way of Jesus. (2) As symbol has transforming effect, so does revelation, introducing us to a new spiritual world, shifting our horizons and views. (3) As symbol has a powerful influence on commitment and behavior, revelation has an impact on the commitments and behavior of those who receive it. (4) As symbol introduces us into realms not normally accessible to discursive thought, "giving rise to thought," revelation gives insight into mysteries that reason cannot fathom (see Avery Dulles, *Models of Revelation* [Garden City, New York: Doubleday, 1983]).

Genuine apparitions are symbolic communications from God, beckoning us to get to know Him, pleading our conversion in thought, behavior, and lifestyle, to lead a new life in response to the call so that we might enjoy the intimate communion in mutual indwelling. These apparitions are obviously not a substitute for absolute faith in God. They are only pointers and signs. We should never lose sight of the object and purpose of God's initiative.

Understandably but unfortunately, there are those who are preoccupied with certain aspects of the phenomena and utilize the popular frenzy to their favor, which can be commercial or ideological or both.

Mary is often portrayed or perceived as a stern judge or a doomsday prophet, rather than a gentle and loving Mother who intercedes for us. It used to be Jesus, as the Pantocrator and the Judge of the world, Who was depicted as severe and almost unapproachable. Now He seems to become too soft. This certainly does not help proper Mariology or ecumenical progress. Mary, as the Mother for all, remains a gentle Mother of the Church, the disciple par excellence, the most attentive and obedient hearer of the Word, thus the dialogue partner of God par excellence.

Here, the eloquent words of Paul VI are still refreshing:

> Contemplated in the episodes of the Gospels and in the reality which she already possesses in the City of God, the Blessed Virgin Mary offers a calm vision and a reassuring word to modern man, torn as he often is between anguish and hope, defeated by his own limitations and assailed by limitless aspirations, troubled in his mind and divided in his heart, uncertain before the riddle of death, oppressed by loneliness while yearning for fellowship, a prey to boredom and disgust. She shows the victory of hope over anguish, of fellowship over solitude, of peace over anxiety, of joy and beauty over boredom and disgust, of eternal vision over earthly ones, of light over death.
>
> — Paul VI, *Marialis Cultus*, No. 57

Not the Y2K, or millennialist, anxiety, but a firm eschatological assurance and hope, namely, that God is in charge through His Son in His Holy Spirit — that is what she brings us in her apparitions.

Desirable Mariological Approach

Why is Mary of help in ecumenical efforts? Obviously first of all, for her special relationship to the Trinity; second, for her special relationship to Jesus Christ; third, because she was present at the beginning of the Church (Calvary and Pentecost).

Mariology must be complete and comprehensive, namely, Trinitarian, Christological, and ecclesial; devotions to Mary must be biblical, liturgical, ecumenical, and anthropological, as recommended by Paul VI (see *Marialis Cultus*, Nos. 24-39; see also *The Virgin Mary in Intellectual and Spiritual Formation*, No. 28). In this way, the person of the Virgin Mary must be considered in the whole of salvation history, that is, in her relation to God the Father; to Christ, the Word Incarnate, Savior and Mediator; to the Holy Spirit, the Sanctifier and Giver of Life; to the human person, in his origin and development in the life of grace, and in his destiny to glory.

This comprehensive approach is to be matched by the following: (1) Return to the sources. (2) Seek knowledge of each other's traditions. (3) Seek common roots of Scripture and patristic writings. (4) Acknowledge legitimate pluralism, such as Pauline Protestant, Johannine Orthodox, Lucan Catholic. (5) Seek to resolve major differences in dogma and devotion. (6) Identify undeveloped themes.

Concluding Remarks

We have learned that Mariology and the Marian devotions, including apparitions, require a comprehensive approach. We need to go beyond sensationalism and sentimentalism, and look out for its exploitation as well.

In terms of the spiritual value of Marian devotions, a genuine Marian piety is to characterize the life of every Christian due to Mary's active presence and role in the history of salvation. In Mary everything is indeed related to Christ; an omission of Marian dimension is quite a loss. While the principle of the hierarchy of truths helps clarify the priority, the potential of popular piety should never be overlooked. Marian apparitions in this context have a potential not only for spiritual nurturing but also for ecumenical progress.

Constant in the ecumenical dialogue on Mary is the scriptural warrant. In fact, this is an ongoing fundamental ecumenical issue. Without oversimplifying the issue, just as there is a danger of false worship of Mary (*Mariolatry*), so there is a danger of a false worship of the Scriptures (*Bibliolatry*). *Sola Scriptura* can be an ideological slogan, thus charged with philosophical presuppositions, which may not be consistent with the mind of those who have discerned them as canonical. Plus, Christianity is not a religion of a book; rather, it is a way of life grounded in the person of Jesus Christ in the Spirit, the Church being the icon of the Trinity. The Weltanschauung, or worldview, of the biblical writers is vastly different from our own, yet their core theological teachings are permanently valid. Each generation has to find a fusion of various horizons to understand and actualize the scriptural revelation, while being open to God's further leading and communication, ready to read the signs of the time.

Marian apparition is one of the signs, certainly not the only sign, which the hearers of the Word of God need to discern and decipher. Not a skeptic, not a zealot, one tries to be a prudent realist.

Indeed the universe is charged with the grandeur of God (Catholic). The cosmos is charged with the mystery of God (Orthodox). All is yours, you are Christ's, and Christ is God's (Protestant). All share the "Christified" horizon. This graced horizon does not limit our vision to the fall and redemption but extends from protology (the study of origins) to eschatology, from creation to fulfillment. The Catholicity with which the

Church is endowed demands that we go beyond our given culture, theology, habits of thought, and conceptual framework to claim all of God's working as ours and to rejoice in them. The catholic (that is, universal) unity has an eschatological outlook without neglecting the proleptic occurrences. Luke's vision is catholic, encompassing history, the powerful and the marginal, women and poor.

"Do whatever he tells you" (Jn 2:5) is the message of Mary yesterday, today, and forever. This is the hallmark of genuine spirituality and Christian behavior and commitments. As the disciples surrounding the Mother received the Holy Spirit, may we follow the Spirit's lead as she always has and always will.

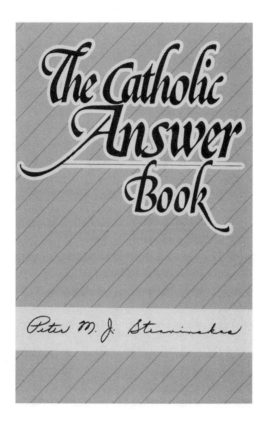

From Catholic history to doctrine to just plain
fascinating facts, you'll find the answers here.
0-87973-**458**-2, paper, $9.95, 192 pp.

To order from Our Sunday Visitor:
Toll free: 1-800-348-2440
E-mail: osvbooks@osv.com
Website: www.osv.com

Prices and availability of books subject to change without notice.

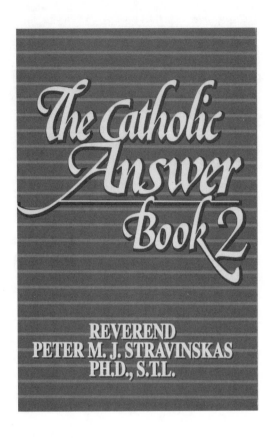

More Catholic questions and answers. Contains
comprehensive index to both volumes.
0-87973-**737**-9, paper, $9.95, 240 pp.

To order from Our Sunday Visitor:
Toll free: 1-800-348-2440
E-mail: osvbooks@osv.com
Website: www.osv.com

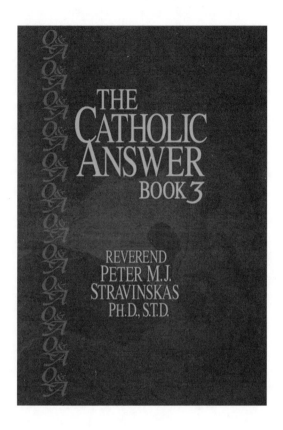

The third in a series, this latest release gives the
definitive Catholic position on many issues.
0-87973-**933**-9, paper, $10.95, 304 pp.

To order from Our Sunday Visitor:
Toll free: 1-800-348-2440
E-mail: osvbooks@osv.com
Website: www.osv.com

Prices and availability of books subject to change without notice.

Our Sunday Visitor. . .
Your Source for Discovering the Riches of the Catholic Faith

Our Sunday Visitor has an extensive line of materials for young children, teens, and adults. Our books, Bibles, booklets, CD-ROMs, audios, and videos are available in bookstores worldwide. To receive a FREE full-line catalog or for more information, call **Our Sunday Visitor** at **1-800-348-2440**. Or write, **Our Sunday Visitor** / 200 Noll Plaza / Huntington, IN 46750.

- -

Please send me: ___A catalog
Please send me materials on:
___Apologetics and catechetics   ___Reference works
___Prayer books   ___Heritage and the saints
___The family   ___The parish
Name_____
Address_____Apt._____
City_____State____Zip_____
Telephone (   ) _____
                                                                            A03BBABP

- -

Please send a friend: ___A catalog
Please send me materials on:
___Apologetics and catechetics   ___Reference works
___Prayer books   ___Heritage and the saints
___The family   ___The parish
Name_____
Address_____Apt._____
City_____State____Zip_____
Telephone (   ) _____
                                                                            A03BBABP

- -

Our Sunday Visitor
200 Noll Plaza
Huntington, IN 46750
Toll free: 1-800-348-2440
E-mail: osvbooks@osv.com
Website: www.osv.com
   Your Source for Discovering the Riches of the Catholic Faith